Quarto.com
© 2024 Quarto Publishing Group USA Inc.
Text © 2024 Meredith Mann

First Published in 2024 by Fair Winds Press, an imprint of The Quarto Group,
100 Cummings Center, Suite 265-D, Beverly, MA 01915, USA.
T (978) 282-9590   F (978) 283-2742

Fair Winds Press titles are also available at discount for retail, wholesale, promotional,
and bulk purchase. For details, contact the Special Sales Manager by email at
specialsales@quarto.com or by mail at The Quarto Group, Attn: Special Sales Manager,
100 Cummings Center, Suite 265-D, Beverly, MA 01915, USA.

28 27 26 25 24   3 4 5

ISBN: 978-0-7603-8740-5
Digital edition published in 2024
eISBN: 978-0-7603-8739-9

Library of Congress Cataloging-in-Publication Data is available.

Design and Page Layout: Laura Shaw Design
Photography: Michelle Miller Photography
Illustration: Abby Winkler

Printed in USA

The information in this book is for educational purposes only. It is not intended
to replace the advice of a physician or medical practitioner. Please see your health-
care provider before beginning any new health program.

The
BLOOD SUGAR
BALANCE
COOKBOOK

---

100 DELICIOUS RECIPES
That Let You Ditch the Crave, Crash, Fat-Storing Cycle
and Heal Your Metabolism

Meredith Mann

Technical Review by Virginia Schilleci, MS, RD, LD

FAIR WINDS

CONTENTS

INTRODUCTION

Welcome to *The Blood Sugar Balance Cookbook*! My name is Meredith Mann. I'm a certified personal trainer, and a certified holistic nutrition coach, specializing in metabolism, fat loss, and emotional eating, and the founder of The Peachie Spoon.

How a Bad Diet Showed Me the Right Way to Eat

I first became aware of the importance of stable blood sugar levels when I started my first diet at 19. But instead of helping me lose weight and feel better, this so-called diet worked against me and my body. In fact, the diet was so restrictive and low-calorie with minimal protein I felt like I was starving. However, I *was* happy thanks to all the compliments I kept getting about my slimmed down body, so I kept on eating this way.

Bottom line? I just wasn't eating enough food, especially protein, which caused my blood sugar levels to drop and left me feeling shaky, anxious, and irritable with intense carb and sugar cravings. This resulted in overeating on "cheat" days which in turn led to feelings of guilt, regret, and remorse about what I'd done.

"I'll start over tomorrow" became my mantra but I felt like I'd failed. Not only was I now imprisoned by my food choices, but I wasn't getting the results that I wanted either. So, I struggled to accept my body as it was, but that wasn't easy either. I stayed in this negative cycle for years.

Ultimately, this led to fainting episodes due to low blood sugar. I was diagnosed by my doctor with hypoglycemia, which meant my blood sugar levels often dropped below a healthy range. For me, it was the blood sugar spike caused by eating an unbalanced meal, the insulin release to control it, and subsequent dive in blood glucose levels that resulted in hypoglycemic symptoms.

Listening to My Body

Once I was diagnosed, I knew that I had to make some big changes. After years of eating the wrong way and feeling unwell, I began to incorporate more whole foods into my diet and started to feel a little better, although, I still experienced dips in my blood sugar levels that caused mood swings, irritability, and binging episodes. At this point I exhibited pre-diabetic/insulin-resistant fasting glucose levels at the doctor when I had my yearly physical.

I just wasn't feeling like myself, and I had three small children to care for. I was either hungry or feeling too full. Food was constantly on my mind. After months, I even tried medication for anxiety and depression. Although the medication helped my mood, the root cause was blood sugar dysregulation. I was in surviving, not thriving mode.

Why Balanced Blood Sugar Matters

My "Ah-ha!" moment came when I figured out the optimal plate balance with a focus on protein and fiber, moderate healthy fats, and carbohydrates to stabilize my blood sugar levels. This prevented the insulin spike that had resulted from eating the wrong foods, and the subsequent dip and low blood sugar that caused so many of my symptoms. With this combination, I was finally able to curb my hunger and cravings, stop overeating, and stop overthinking what I put into my mouth. Eating this way also helped to stabilize my mood. It was an amazing shift!

The bonus? I realized that there were numerous health benefits that came from keeping my blood sugar in balance. It helped to restore my metabolism, lower inflammation, and gradually lose weight in a healthy way and keep it off.

Sharing My Experiences with Others

Discovering this new way of eating changed my life, and I wanted to share my knowledge with others which is why I started my Instagram (@thepeachiespoon) in 2019. My goal? To show my followers why balanced blood sugar matters and to share simple ways to make it a habit while feeding their family well too.

The first recipe I posted was a yummy blood sugar friendly smoothie recipe that contained protein, healthy fats, fiber, and even a serving of carbohydrates. Not only was it a nourishing breakfast but it also curbed my afternoon cravings, which was a game changer for me.

I was excited to share this recipe because it was full of the nutrients that my body had so desperately needed when I tried my first diet. Back then, my body had been crying out for nourishment, and overeating was the only way I knew to address this problem. I then came to know better and was eager to help others improve their health and well-being too.

Soon after, The Peachie Spoon blossomed into a full-time coaching business and recipe blog. It's because of my personal experience that I'm so passionate about helping people choose and prepare foods that simplify eating, improve health, provide energy, and help us care for ourselves and those we love.

Today, I love creating simple family-friendly recipes that nourish the body, stabilize blood sugar levels, and help you to feel your best.

I'm so grateful you're here!

—Meredith

1

What Is Blood Sugar Balance & Why Does It Matter?

TO KEEP IT SIMPLE, your blood glucose level refers to the concentration of glucose (a type of sugar) in your bloodstream. Glucose levels and blood sugar levels mean the same thing. Keep in mind, blood sugar levels and responses to foods are always individual and vary from person to person.

Certain foods like white bread, white rice, and simple carbs—think cookies and candy—ramp up blood sugar levels. This triggers the body to release insulin which causes blood sugar levels to drop. When this process is repeated over and over, it can result in hypoglycemia, a condition in which your blood sugar crashes too low, which is what happened to me.

However, when we eat the right foods, like complex carbs, healthy fats, fiber, and protein, our bodies don't have to work so hard. Foods like cruciferous and root vegetables; proteins from meat, eggs, and some dairy if tolerated; sprouted or high-quality grains; and fruit can all be part of a blood sugar friendly plate.

When we eat the right way, our blood sugar is naturally in balance, we can maintain a healthy weight and we have sustained energy to do the things we want and need to do. You can think of these foods as fuel for a car; when we have what we need in the tank, we function better, feel good, and improve health and wellness.

Blood sugar balance is also critical for maintaining overall health and wellness. That's because when dysregulated blood sugar levels become routine, it puts stress on your body.

It's not just diabetics that deal with this issue either. New studies show that 88 percent of non-diabetics have imbalanced blood sugar on a regular basis and they may not even know it. (See https://www.ncbi.nlm.nih.gov/pmc/articles/PMC4116271/ for more information.) Symptoms of blood sugar imbalance can include intense cravings, anxiety, mood swings, frequent urination, and weight gain.

Chronic Blood Sugar Imbalance Is a Contributing Factor to Inflammatory Diseases and More

Over time, chronic blood sugar dysregulation can contribute to inflammatory diseases like type 2 diabetes, heart disease, and Alzheimer's. Blood sugar fluctuations create a cascade effect of inflammatory damage to the body's cells, tissues, and organs.

HEART Chronic inflammation can damage the lining of the blood vessels and increase the formation of plaques that can block blood flow and cause heart attacks or strokes.

DIABETES Chronic inflammation can impair the function of insulin, a hormone that regulates blood sugar levels and causes insulin resistance. This can lead to high blood sugar levels and diabetes.

CANCER Chronic inflammation can cause DNA damage, cell mutations, and abnormal cell growth that can lead to cancer. Inflammation can also promote the spread of cancer cells and interfere with the immune system's ability to fight them.

BRAIN Chronic inflammation can affect the brain and nervous system and cause cognitive decline, memory loss, and dementia. Inflammation can also contribute to the development of diseases such as Alzheimer's, Parkinson's, and multiple sclerosis.

AUTOIMMUNE Chronic inflammation can cause the immune system to attack the body's own tissues and organs, resulting in autoimmune diseases such as rheumatoid arthritis, lupus, psoriasis, and inflammatory bowel disease.

As you can see, dysregulated blood sugar affects so many aspects of our health. That's why it's absolutely vital to get our breakfast, lunch, dinner, and snack plates in balance.

Blood Sugar Imbalance, Metabolism, and Weight Loss

Imbalanced blood sugar not only causes this inflammatory cascade; it also impacts how we burn and store body fat. Burning fat is not just about how you look physically. Having better metabolic health equals more energy, better hormonal health, lower risk of heart disease, and so much more.

Insulin, the hormone that regulates our blood sugar, also signals the body to store calories as fat. So, if your insulin is always elevated, it is going to be very challenging for you to burn fat and lose weight. When blood sugar is balanced, insulin is low, metabolic rate increases, and fat cells get smaller.

If you are eating a low-calorie diet, but your meals are still not focused on blood sugar balance, you can still lose weight because you are in a caloric deficit. However, you'll also be losing muscle, bone mass, and water weight with minimal fat loss because your insulin is high.

Losing muscle, bone mass, and water can leave you with a slower metabolic rate, pre-osteoporosis, and a dehydrated body. Losing weight long term can become even more challenging, and over time can create other health issues.

Aging Impacts Blood Sugar Balance Too

Age is another factor that makes you more sensitive to weight gain and imbalanced blood sugar. As we age, we naturally lose muscle mass, usually starting around the age of 30. This matters because blood sugar balance is closely tied to the amount of muscle you have. We store 80 percent of our glucose (carbs) in our muscles and the remainder in our liver. When these two storage spaces are full, you begin to store glucose in fat cells, like a savings account for a rainy day.

The problem is that most people already have plenty in savings already and don't need to add to their fat stores. So, to put it simply, more muscle equals more energy storage space for glucose, which means fewer blood sugar spikes, fewer insulin spikes, and usually that means less weight gain.

To build muscle, it's smart to add weight and resistance training to your exercise routine along with eating enough protein. But also include exercise you enjoy, whether it's walking, swimming, yoga, or another activity. If you like doing it, you'll do it more often and more consistently.

Another age-related factor that impacts blood sugar is perimenopause and menopause. As we age, we naturally have higher insulin levels, or we become insulin resistant because insulin is regulated by estrogen and progesterone. When these sex hormones decrease, as they normally do during perimenopause and menopause, your cells become more resistant to insulin.

Sleep disturbances which often result from these hormonal fluctuations are also a factor. Lack of sleep affects your hunger hormones and appetite, making it even harder for your body to regulate blood sugar levels. This is why our weight balance depends on so much more than calories in and calories out, especially as we age.

The Plate Structure Solution: Blood Sugar Stabilizing Meals and Snacks

I created an optimal balance plate structure for each meal to keep blood sugar stable and steady. It's composed of protein, fat, and fiber, with one optional serving of carbohydrate (or carbs) per meal.

This structure means that you'll fill your plate with 50 percent of non-starchy vegetables for fiber, one quarter of your plate with protein, and the other quarter with an optional fist-size serving of a carbohydrate food, if desired. Carbs like fruit, potatoes, or bread affect blood sugar balance, so keeping this aspect to a fist-size serving per meal helps to keep levels stable without having to count grams of carbs.

Remember, it's a gentle structure and not rigid. Healing blood sugar dysregulation does not have to be difficult or complicated. All foods can fit on your plate to make this approach doable long term.

I know my optimal plate balance works because it's worked for me and thousands of my clients over the years. Following this approach prevented further hypoglycemia (preventing the blood sugar spike meant no more crashes or low blood sugar) and improved my fasting glucose levels. Before I employed these strategies, I was always in the 100–110 range. (See https://www.ncbi.nlm.nih.gov/pmc/articles/PMC2769652/ for more information.) Now, I personally stay in the 75–110 range most of the time.

THE BALANCED PLATE

Fiber (vegetables)

Starch/Carbs (optional)

Protein and Fat
*add more fat if lean protein

If you want more individual data for yourself, try using a continuous glucose monitor (CGM). It can be eye opening to see how certain foods affect you and motivate you to make healthier choices that balance your blood sugar levels.

You deserve to live your best and most energetic life. The good news is healthy eating doesn't have to be difficult. All the recipes in this book are simple and designed to balance your blood sugar. Most of your favorite foods will fit somewhere on your plate if you follow my guidelines. Let's give a hand for food freedom, healthy eating, and peace of mind!

The Strategy and Science of Creating a Blood Sugar Balanced Meal

There is a strategy and science to the plate structure and eating meals that are in balance, and much of that is based on how your body works to break down and metabolize food.

By following more of a balanced plate method, you can stabilize your hunger hormones, turn on your satiety hormones, and consistently balance your blood sugar. When you eat, your body breaks down carbs into glucose for energy, proteins into amino acids that are carried to tissues and organs, and fats into fatty acids to store energy, insulate us, and act as messengers to help proteins do their job.

As you can see, each nutrient is vital. From a blood sugar standpoint, carbs, especially ones from sugar and processed grains, raise blood sugar rapidly. While proteins, fats, and fiber have a slower and lower impact on blood sugar. It's all about balance.

The Four Hunger Hormones and What They Do

Science tells us that there are four hormones that dictate our appetite. Each of these has a specific job and will tell you if you are hungry or full and satisfied. When you don't enable these hormones to act effectively, problems arise.

The Standard American Diet (or SAD because of its heavy inclusion of refined sugars and processed foods) can throw these hunger hormones out of whack. When these hormones are not firing properly, you aren't getting accurate hunger and satiety signals. This means that your body can't accurately recognize when to eat and when to stop. Often, this is the result of chronic blood sugar imbalance. Let's take a close look at the four hunger hormones.

INSULIN

Insulin is released from the pancreas after you eat to capture blood sugar and store it for energy in your liver, muscles, and fat cells. If you have a more blood sugar friendly meal, like protein and vegetables, your hunger hormones will be stabilized, carbs will be stored for quick energy in your liver and muscles, and you will experience calm hunger about 3–5 hours after a meal. This is opposed to the panicked, "hangry" kind of hunger 1–2 hours after eating that you will tend to experience when you are riding a blood sugar rollercoaster.

When you eat too many carbs at once, or a not-so-balanced meal or snack, like a big bowl of oatmeal topped with honey and fruit, or a fruit-filled smoothie without protein and healthy fats added, your blood sugar will spike and then quickly drop too low and crash. The result? Your brain and body will crave more carbs and sugar (hormonal hunger, not a true hunger) for energy to bring it back to balance.

At the same time, your liver and muscles are full of stored glucose from the earlier spike, so any other carbs eaten soon after can be stored as a savings account of fuel in your fat cells. Slowly but surely, you gain more body fat. Do you see how these spikes and crashes can easily become your norm?

They certainly were for me. I felt hungry all the time and could not stop thinking about food. This all changed for me when I created the balanced plate structure solution for each meal. When you put it into practice by using the simple recipes in this book for breakfast, lunch, dinner, and snacks, you'll immediately begin to store energy in your liver and muscles more than in your fat cells. You'll have the right balance of carbs from fiber-rich veggies and the optional fist-size serving of carbs for healthy energy and fuel, but you'll be out of the dreaded fat-storing zone.

Insulin Resistance

Let's talk about insulin resistance, or pre-diabetes, which is a condition where blood sugar levels are high, but not high enough to be classified as type 2 diabetes. This condition can be reversed but not without a shift in what you choose to eat and other lifestyle factors like exercise. If changes aren't implemented, this can shift to type 2 diabetes.

Insulin resistance or pre-diabetes is what happens when your blood sugar is repeatedly out of balance due to your food choices. When the insulin in your body is chronically elevated, your cells can become resistant to it. This means it's no longer as effective at regulating glucose in your body and keeping your blood sugar stable.

Imagine that insulin is the key that helps open the door to our cells so that glucose can get inside and give us energy. If you have insulin resistance, the lock on the door gets a bit rusty. This means that the key (insulin) has a harder time opening the door and glucose can't get into our cells as easily.

When this happens, our body must work overtime and begin to produce more insulin to try to open the door. To avoid insulin resistance, we need to keep the lock on our cells working well by eating a healthy balance of nutrients. That way, the key (insulin) can do its job properly.

Insulin Resistance and Metabolic Flexibility

Metabolic flexibility is the process by which your body switches between different sources of fuel for energy, whether it's glucose or fatty acids. Often, insulin resistance can lead to metabolic inflexibility because your body is blocking the absorption of glucose as a fuel source which leaves you craving carbs. When you're insulin sensitive and can maintain optimal insulin levels, this allows your body to be metabolically flexible.

Think of your body as if it functioned like a hybrid car, meaning it can run on different energy sources. In the case of the car, it's either gas or electricity. When it comes to your body, it's glucose or fatty acids. Metabolic flexibility is like the hybrid car that seamlessly switches between different energy sources, depending on what's available and needed. This means you still feel okay, even if a meal is delayed, because your body can switch to a different fuel source and create energy.

Insulin Sensitivity

You can see why when it comes to balanced blood sugar, the goal is for our cells to be sensitive to insulin. This means that the key fits into the door to your cells, opens, and allows glucose to enter so that you can get the energy you need. It's a good thing when our cells are insulin-sensitive because it helps maintain stable blood sugar levels, reduces the risk of type 2 diabetes, and makes you feel more energetic and healthier so you can more easily live out your life's purpose and passions.

When you strengthen insulin sensitivity through a balanced diet, regular exercise, and a healthy lifestyle, which includes good sleep hygiene and stress management, you keep the key (insulin) and the cell door in tip-top shape. This ensures your body functions the way it should. It also means lower body fat and more fat burning time overnight and between meals because insulin is lower overall.

Three other hunger hormones—glucagon, leptin, and ghrelin—work with insulin to regulate your appetite and keep blood glucose levels in balance.

GLUCAGON

Glucagon is a hormone that primarily raises your blood sugar if it drops too low, but it can't be released if there's insulin present. So, when your blood sugar levels are low, maybe because you haven't eaten for a while, glucagon steps in and tells your liver to release some stored sugar aka glycogen. The liver turns this secret stash of sugar into glucose and sends it to your blood stream for energy until food is available and gives us a "chill" slow hunger signal.

So, if you're eating a lot of carbs, or habitually snacking or grazing, and you don't give your body a break between meals so that insulin levels can return to normal, insulin levels will be consistently high so you're unable to use glucagon.

Some experts suggest that you should eat small balanced snacks every 2–3 hours to keep blood sugar stable. But this is only a Band-Aid to help blood sugar levels because it still results in insulin working overtime with spikes and crashes all day long.

Glucagon also can't do its job which is to act as your body's natural fat-burning mechanism. High levels of insulin also result in that "hangry" feeling. In addition, even if you aren't consuming many calories, you'll still be unable to lose fat. This is what happens with diets that severely restrict calories without enough protein.

LEPTIN

Leptin is our satiety hormone. It's a hormone derived from the adipose tissue and small intestines and helps to suppress hunger. It gives our brain that, "Hey, I'm feeling good and nourished" feeling for 4–5 hours after a meal.

However, problems can arise when you have chronically high insulin levels. The leptin signals don't fire off correctly, leading to leptin resistance. In other words, your brain isn't getting that "I'm comfortably full, let's stop eating" signal. This means it can be impossible to feel satisfied, which can lead to overeating too many calories and unwanted weight gain or obesity.

GHRELIN

Ghrelin is our "tummy rumbles" hormone. It tells us when it's time to eat. It's produced mostly by the stomach with small amounts released by the pancreas, brain, and small intestine. Ghrelin stimulates appetite, increases food intake, and promotes fat storage.

Fixing the Problem: Eating a Balanced Meal with My Plate Structure Solution

The solution to achieving blood sugar balance and enabling these four hormones to do their jobs is eating a balanced meal. Yes, it really is that simple. Keep in mind that a balanced meal does not mean crazy restrictive zero carb diets, zero fat, good or bad food lists, or having to count every macronutrient in an app. It just means using my easy-to-follow optimal plate structure solution.

Everything you need to help the hunger hormones do their jobs and nourish your body will fit on your plate. This means this system is not only simple, but it'll also make healthy eating a lifetime habit. Once you're able to maintain stable blood sugar levels, you'll experience fewer cravings, banish overeating, and finally find food freedom.

You'll also finally be eating in a way that supports your metabolism rather than works against it. Trust me, you don't need another extreme diet. You just need to break the cycle of blood sugar dysregulation one simple meal at a time.

Macronutrients & Blood Sugar Balance

MACRONUTRIENTS INCLUDE protein, carbs, and fat. But I also include fiber in my optimal plate structure solution because it's just so vital from a blood sugar balance standpoint. Each macronutrient is of equal importance, and understanding how they work together is essential when it comes to effectively managing blood glucose levels.

Keep in mind that the precise ratio of protein, carbs, fiber, and fats should be tailored to your individual health goals and dietary needs. This is true whether your goal is stabilizing your blood glucose levels, losing weight, or if you have specific health conditions that demand special attention. So, it's a good idea to consult with your health care practitioner or registered dietitian to help determine the optimal macronutrient distribution for you.

Protein: Why It Should Be the Star of Your Plate

Protein is the most important nutrient when it comes to balancing blood glucose levels. However, it is also an essential building block of bones and muscles, helps detox your liver, and repairs tissues in the body like cartilage, organs, and skin. Protein helps to speed exercise recovery and healing from injuries.

Protein can also help reduce muscle loss which occurs naturally as we age. This is important because our muscles play an essential role when it comes to stabilizing blood sugar levels. That's because most of our glucose is stored in our muscles, and only a small amount is stored in the liver. Having muscle helps to regulate blood sugar levels. Simply put, more skeletal muscle equals more glucose storage, which can mean more stable blood sugar.

Protein is a very versatile micronutrient. It has the highest thermogenic effect of any nutrient, which means that calories are burned faster when they are broken down and digested by the body. Although carbs and fats are the primary sources of energy, if needed, the body can use protein too.

Keep in mind that protein must be eaten, the body can't make protein on its own. This is one reason why it's the primary focus of my balanced plate structure.

PROTEIN AND BLOOD SUGAR BALANCE

Compared to complex carbs, protein has a slow and more gradual effect on blood glucose levels. So, you won't feel the results of this important macronutrient instantaneously. This is because protein needs to be broken down into amino acids before it can be absorbed into the bloodstream and assimilated by the body.

Certain amino acids derived from protein such as alanine, arginine, and asparagine can be converted directly into glucose through a process called gluconeogenesis. This is when your body makes new glucose from protein and fat when no carbs are ingested and you're out of glucose stores for easy energy. Typically, though, this process only occurs if you are fasting or on an extreme low-carb diet and the body needs glucose for energy.

When gluconeogenesis is triggered, it is a stress response produced by the body. It's your body's response to produce fuel (glucose) when it's otherwise not available, like eating very low-carb. It's amazing our bodies can do this! We are so well made, but extreme low-carb diets can affect energy levels overtime because this process is "extra work" for our bodies if done all the time.

On the other hand, protein-rich foods fill you up and help control your appetite. They also reduce the craving for high-carbohydrate or sugary foods, which can cause a rapid spike in blood sugar. In this way, protein-rich foods stabilize blood sugar levels, meal to meal, day to day.

If you have any specific concerns regarding how protein may impact your blood sugar, it's a good idea to discuss this with your health care practitioner or registered dietitian. Either can offer personalized guidance tailored to your unique dietary requirements and make sure that your diet aligns with your overall health goals.

The Good News about Fat and Why You Need It

Despite what you may think, not all fats are bad. Good fats found in nuts, seeds, fruit, and fruit oils like olive, coconut, and avocado offer a wide range of health benefits and belong on your plate. These fats help protect your heart, reduce inflammation, form a crucial part of the cell membrane, and help maintain cellular function.

These fats also help the body absorb fat-soluble vitamins including A, D, E, and K. Omega-3 fatty acids help improve brain function and overall cognitive health. Fats play a role in the production of sex hormones like estrogen and testosterone and help maintain hormonal balance. Fat also acts as an energy storage system. This means that if you need energy, and carbs are not available, fat can do the job.

HOW FAT AFFECTS BLOOD SUGAR BALANCE

Unlike carbs, that can quickly affect blood sugar levels, fat is digested more slowly which means it has less impact. This means that when you add healthy fats with each meal, it will help delay the absorption of carbs, which leads to a slow and more gradual increase in blood sugar levels.

Foods that are naturally abundant in healthy fats have the beneficial effect of promoting a sense of fullness and satiety. These fats include avocados, olives, grass-fed meats, chicken thighs, monounsaturated and polyunsaturated fats found in extra virgin olive oil, grass-fed butter, egg yolks, fatty fish (think SMASH: salmon, mackerel, anchovies, sardines, and herring), and nuts. When we feel satisfied, we can better manage portion control and maintain more consistent blood sugar levels over time.

On the other hand, trans fats and excessive saturated fats found in margarine, seed oils, canola oil, vegetable oils, fried foods, commercial baked goods, and shortening should be limited in the diet due to their adverse effects on heart health. Moderation in the consumption of saturated fats is recommended for the sake of overall cardiovascular well-being. Choosing healthy fats and avoiding bad fats can make a significant impact on your blood sugar and overall health and well-being.

For personalized advice on managing dietary fat in terms of blood sugar balance, especially if you have specific dietary concerns, please see your health care practitioner or dietitian for dietary recommendations.

Eating for Blood Sugar Balance: Let's Talk about Carbs

As a macronutrient, carbs have the most direct impact on blood sugar levels and whether it is in or out of balance. When you eat carbs, your body breaks them down into glucose (sugar), which is then released into the blood stream. This leads to an increase in blood sugar levels. The rate and extent of this rise depends on several factors, including the type of carbs and the presence of other nutrients like fiber, fat, and protein.

SIMPLE VS. COMPLEX CARBOHYDRATES: CHOOSE WISELY

The type of carbs you choose to eat matters when it comes to blood sugar balance. Simple carbs constructed of simple sugar molecules are found in soda, juices and energy drinks, candy, cookies, and other sugar-laden snacks. These carbs are quickly digested and can cause rapid blood sugar spikes, increased insulin, and the crash that follows. So, moderation is important when it comes to these types of foods.

Complex carbs, on the other hand, found in whole grains, vegetables, and legumes, are composed of longer chain sugar molecules that are digested more slowly thanks to the fiber they contain. This means a gradual and more manageable rise in blood sugar levels that makes us feel our best. Fiber is also vital for digestive health, helps you feel full, and regulates blood sugar levels.

Complex carbs are our body's preferred energy source because this macronutrient is easily transformed into glucose and ready to use. Our brains primarily run on glucose, which is essential for optimal brain function and cognitive performance. This shows you just how important this nutrient can be.

In addition, carbs provide fuel and energy for muscles when you're active or exercising. This macronutrient also prevents protein from being used as a last resort energy source, which stresses the body and instead allows it to do its work building and maintaining muscle strength.

AN INDIVIDUAL APPROACH TO CARB INTAKE

Our activity levels, metabolism, sleep quality, and hormones all play a big role in deter-mining our carb intake and what works best for us, so maintaining blood sugar balance is different for everyone. In the simplest terms, carbs and starches affect blood glucose levels the same way, so keeping them in the same category on your plate, and to one optional serving per meal, makes sense.

However, if you're young, an athlete, pregnant, nursing, or doing intense workouts five or more times a week, you may need more than one serving per meal of complex carbs for muscle recovery and a healthy body, especially post workout. For most everyone else, I've found that the balanced plate structure solution including one optional carbohydrate/starch per meal works well.

That said, keep in mind that if you're a woman in perimenopause or menopause, or have pre-diabetes, insulin resistance, or metabolic syndrome, your insulin will be naturally higher. This means you may want to skip your carbohydrate/starch at some meals. Experiment with what makes you feel your best.

Patients with Type 1 and 2 diabetes mellitus should work closely with their physician or registered dietitian when managing their diet.

You can see that everyone has different health and nutritional needs when it comes to carbs. Some individuals may be more sensitive to carb intake, while others may have greater tolerance or need more depending on their lifestyle. This is why I always stress the importance of personalized blood sugar management.

The bottom line? The relationship between carbs and blood sugar is an important one. Being mindful of your carb intake, making informed food choices, and practicing portion control are all key strategies when it comes to balanced blood sugar levels.

Consulting with a health care practitioner or registered dietitian is also smart because it will help you develop your own individualized approach to carbs that aligns with your specific dietary needs and overall health and wellness goals.

The Many Benefits of Fiber

Although fiber is not considered one of the "main" macronutrients like protein, fat, and carbs, it is important for good nutrition, blood sugar balance, and more. High-fiber foods tend to be more filling, which can help control your appetite, reduce cravings, and curb overeating.

Fiber can help lower LDL cholesterol levels, blood pressure, and inflammation. It also helps prevent constipation and promotes a healthy gut microbiome. That's because fiber contains prebiotics that contribute to beneficial bacteria growth in the colon, which supports overall health.

Probiotics are good bacteria that have a beneficial effect on your body. Prebiotics, found in fibrous foods, are food for the probiotics in your body. They help to fight off the less friendly or "bad" bacteria and can boost your immune system against infections.

FIBER AND BLOOD SUGAR BALANCE

Not only does fiber contribute to balanced blood sugar levels, it also helps to reduce spikes. There are two types of fiber: soluble and insoluble. Soluble fiber means that it dissolves in water and forms a gel-like substance in the digestive tract. This slows the absorption of glucose from the digestive system, which helps to prevent rapid blood sugar spikes after a meal.

Foods rich in soluble fiber include psyllium husk, vegetables like Brussels sprouts, turnips, and broccoli, and carbohydrate-rich sources like beans, sweet potatoes, lentils, and fruits. Insoluble fiber adds bulk to stool and aids in digestion and elimination. Although it doesn't have a direct impact on blood sugar like soluble fiber, it still contributes to gastrointestinal and overall health.

Incorporating fiber-rich foods into your diet along with other macronutrients and monitoring your carb intake are strategies that will help you successfully manage your blood sugar levels. However, it's important to introduce dietary changes gradually, especially when it comes to your fiber intake. Eating too much fiber, too often, can lead to gastrointestinal upset. Your body will need time to adjust to a new way of eating.

If you have specific dietary concerns regarding fiber and optimizing blood sugar balance, seek guidance from a health care practitioner or registered dietitian. A professional can help tailor a personalized plan that works just for you.

Blood Sugar Hacks

Easy Ways to Maintain Blood Sugar Balance

IN THIS CHAPTER, you'll find tools, tweaks, and short-cuts to make it easier to keep your blood sugar in balance. This will help you make keeping your blood sugar stable a habit and part of your daily routine. Although these tips aren't medical treatments or cures, you'll find them useful as you begin your journey to healthy blood glucose management.

Keep in mind that these hacks are to empower you with useful and usable information, not overwhelm you by adding to your to-do list. Stress can trigger inflammation as much as blood sugar spikes do, so I've tried to make these hacks easy to do.

My motto is: Wellness without Obsession. It's always important to balance knowledge that empowers you with rest, rejuvenation, and recovery.

Remember that what works for someone else may not work for you, and not all "life hacks" are supported by scientific research. That said, sometimes common sense can be the best way forward. So, choose tips, tools, and hacks that make sense to you and will help you in your journey to healthy blood sugar levels.

Eat Food in the Right Order

When you sit down to eat, look at your plate. Did you know that it matters which foods you eat first, second, and third? It does. What you eat, when, can help the body absorb glucose more slowly, reduce insulin release, and balance blood sugar levels. I've found that the optimal order of macronutrients you eat should be in this order: first fiber, think colorful veggies, next protein, fat, and finally complex carbs.

Why is this important? When we eat fiber first, especially before carbs, starches, and sugars, it lines the stomach, which reduces and slows down the absorption of glucose. Protein does too, so eating this first not only helps you feel full, it keeps your blood sugar balanced.

Eating the same exact meal, in a different order, can give a completely different blood sugar response for some. Of course, if you make a smoothie with every macronutrient, they're absorbed all at once, and the combination can help ensure blood sugar that stays in balance.

For example, one day while I was making my smoothie for breakfast, I popped a couple of fresh delicious strawberries in my mouth. I thought this was no big deal because I was about to have a smoothie full of fiber, healthy fats, and plenty of protein a few minutes later.

But eating those strawberries without anything else gave me a huge sugar spike on my continuous glucose monitor (CGM) that I wasn't expecting, which led to a crash and symptoms including racing heart, anxiety, and feeling sleepy followed by carb cravings. This was my reaction, and it won't be the same for everyone. Still, it does show that eating foods in optimal order matters.

This doesn't mean that you must be regimented and eat all your chicken and broccoli before you touch your potato. It's more about being mindful of what's on your plate and trying to eat foods in the optimal order for blood sugar balance. For example, you may want to have a couple bites of broccoli and chicken before you dive into that yummy potato.

Here's a good example of how the order of what you eat affects appetite. Think about that bread basket that was put on the table the last time you visited your favorite restaurant. This isn't an accident. Eating white bread will trigger a sugar spike and insulin response that will make you feel hungrier. This means that you'll order more food, which can mean a higher tab for your meal.

Bread isn't off limits entirely. Just be mindful and set a piece aside and enjoy it after your salad or appetizer or with your meal which probably contains protein. The same goes for dessert. Yes, grandma was right. Dessert should be eaten after a meal, not as a snack, especially if you want to keep your blood sugar stable.

The Benefits of Exercise: Get Moving!

Physical activity, even in the form of a short walk, can enhance your body's sensitivity to insulin. When your cells become more receptive to insulin, it means that they can better process glucose from the blood stream, which leads to more stable blood sugar levels after you eat. Moving your body also makes more room in your muscles to store excess glucose in your bloodstream and prevent a post meal spike.

As a rule of thumb, aim for 10–15 minutes of physical activity within 30 minutes to two hours after finishing a meal. Even light physical activity like a walk can help the digestive process and stabilize blood sugar. Of course, there will be days when you just feel like flopping on the couch after a meal. That's okay and there's no reason to feel guilty. Rest, and then try to get moving again. What's important is consistency, not perfection.

Skip "Naked" Carbs

Eating naked or high-carbohydrate foods like sweets, white bread, white pasta, or cake, especially when not a part of a balanced meal containing protein, fat, and fiber, will spike blood sugar levels for most people. You'll be up thanks to the quick hit of sugar and just as quickly enter an energy slump that will trigger cravings for more carbs. It's a vicious cycle.

Instead, when we pair complex carbs with healthy fats, protein, and fiber, it slows the digestion and absorption of glucose, leading to more stable blood sugar and fewer cravings. Did I mention you'll also feel much better? Choosing say, an apple, which contains fiber, as a healthy snack is a much better option. Even better, pair it with some cheese or nut butter, so you're adding healthy fats and some protein too.

Sleep and Blood Sugar Balance

Sleep matters when it comes to blood sugar balance. So, it's important to make it a priority to get between seven and nine hours each night. When you don't get enough sleep, it can cause the cells in your body to become insulin resistant, which boosts blood sugar levels. Poor sleep can also mean more stress and raised cortisol levels which can also affect blood sugar. Inflammation and oxidative stress are exacerbated by poor sleep, and this too can impact glucose levels and your insulin sensitivity.

The other three hunger hormones—glucagon, leptin, and ghrelin—are affected too. This can lead to cravings for high-carb foods. Even though what you really need is a good night's sleep, your body and brain want energy, and high carbs are the quickest, and not healthiest, way to get it.

Ideally, when you sleep well, the liver naturally releases small amounts of glucose into the bloodstream for a steady supply of energy. However, when sleep patterns are disrupted, this triggers a process known as gluconeogenesis, where we form new sugar as fuel. Stressors to the body can lead to out-of-balance blood sugar levels.

Making good sleep hygiene a priority will aid in maintaining stable blood sugar and proper rest, which directly affects health and well-being.

USE THESE TIPS FOR A BETTER SLEEP

> Establish regular bed and wake times.
> Don't watch or read the news or other stressful content before going to bed.
> Take a warm bath with lavender essential oils and 1 cup of epsom salt to release stress and prepare your body and brain for sleep.
> Make sure the bedroom is cool or at a temperature that promotes sleep.
> Use Blue Shade on your devices to prepare your brain for sleep.
> If a bright bedroom wakes you up, install room darkening shades.
> Don't work in the bedroom or do bills. Keep it a place for sleep, sex, and relaxation.

Managing Stress for Better Blood Sugar Balance

Feeling stressed or overwhelmed can affect your body's ability to regulate blood sugar levels. When you feel stressed, the body releases hormones such as cortisol and adrenaline. These stress hormones elevate blood sugar levels that tell the liver to release glucose into the bloodstream for energy so you can fight or flee. For example, I've noticed a blood sugar spike on my GSM (glucose monitoring device) when I'm feeling stressed before public speaking engagements.

Our bodies have been designed to handle some stress. After all, it's part of daily life. The problem occurs when stress becomes chronic, and the body is triggered into this response repeatedly. Chronic stress can wreak havoc on blood sugar levels and make it more difficult to bring them back into balance, even if you're eating right and exercising.

For this reason, it's important to include practices to reduce stress such as slow and measured breathing, deep belly breathing, meditation, yoga, yoga nidra, and mindfulness that promotes relaxation. Apps like Calm make it easy. You can also find many audiobooks with guided meditations that help ease stress.

When you incorporate stress relief into your day, you short circuit the fight or flight response and move into a more relaxed way of being. Not only is this important in terms of blood sugar management, it's also very good for your overall health. Stress often contributes to numerous chronic illnesses.

You may also want to consider rethinking your priorities and goals, boundaries with other people, and even saying "no" to requests if you feel stressed and overwhelmed. When you take care of yourself and your own mental health, you're better able to care for others.

If you feel depressed or anxious, you may want to consider talking to a therapist. It can be a relief to have a safe space to share your concerns and problems and find solutions. PsychologyToday.com has listings for all types of therapists who can help you feel better.

Using a holistic approach that combines stress management along with a balanced diet and exercise all contribute to stable blood sugar control and give your body what it needs to relax and recover.

THE RECIPES

BALANCED BLOOD SUGAR MADE EASY

All of the recipes in this book feature my balanced plate structure solution and include portions of protein, fat, fiber, and an optional carbohydrate/starch. You'll find this helpful, especially if you don't want to count macros or calories but would like to be aware of the categories that each recipe features. That said, you'll also find macro counts to guide you, along with serving suggestions.

I've tested all of these recipes on myself while wearing a continuous glucose monitor (CGM). You may want to experiment with different recipes while wearing a CGM to fine-tune which ones work best for you in terms of your blood sugar balance needs. It's interesting to see what's happening to your blood sugar levels in real time, and the feedback is useful for planning meals.

BABY STEPS + CONSISTENCY = PROGRESS

Remember that with each balanced meal that you prepare and eat, you're improving your health and wellness one baby step at a time. Keep in mind that all or nothing thinking when eating a new way sets you up for failure. So instead, aim for progress, not perfection. This isn't a diet, it's an eating plan that simplifies managing blood sugar levels.

Once eating this new way becomes a habit, you'll notice that maintaining balanced blood sugar makes you feel better and gives you more energy. Over time you'll be able to tell if you've eaten too much sugar or carbs by the way you feel, without a glucose monitor. If you do overeat, make a mistake, or have a setback, don't get down on yourself. Instead, learn from the experience and use it to move forward in a positive direction.

My hope is that these recipes will get you excited about eating well, and encourage you to experience the joy of cooking, dining, and sharing meals with loved ones around the table. Balancing blood sugar levels through a new way of eating can be truly transformative and contribute to an enhanced sense of well-being and an improved quality of life.

4

Breakfast

BREAKFAST is the most important meal of the day. But it matters what kind of breakfast you choose. Eating a breakfast of sugary cereals, pastries, and other high-sugar, low-nutrient options will guarantee a day of hunger, cravings, and overeating. Choosing macronutrients like protein, healthy fats, and complex carbs will give you nourishment and energy while balancing your blood sugar levels and improving your mood.

Protein Cheesecake Parfait

This one is great as a meal prep if you double or triple the recipe. It adds variety to breakfast too, while stabilizing blood sugar. Skip the nuts and it's a healthy dessert option after a meal.

½ cup (115 g) low-fat cottage cheese

2 tablespoons (30 g) nonfat Greek yogurt

½ teaspoon vanilla extract

½ teaspoon cinnamon, optional

1 ounce (16 g) vanilla or chocolate protein

⅓ cup (42 g) desired berries, fresh or frozen

2 tablespoons (32 g) nut butter of choice or desired nuts for a crunch

Place cottage cheese, yogurt, vanilla extract, cinnamon (if desired), and protein powder in a blender or food processor and blend until smooth.

Layer half the mixture, then half the berries and nuts, then the other half of the mixture, and top with remaining berries and nuts or nut butter for healthy fats.

Store in the fridge. Good for a week.

Per serving with 2 tablespoons peanut butter (32 g) and fresh raspberries
396 calories • 18 g fat • 16 g carbs • 6 g fiber • 36 g protein

Nourishment Breakdown

PROTEIN powder, yogurt, cottage cheese	FAT nuts FIBER some in berries	CARB/STARCH berries

Pesto Protein Egg Muffins

These are great for the whole family and contain 30 g protein to stabilize blood sugar. Try eating these with a piece of fruit on the go to start your day. My kids like them with a waffle or toast in the morning.

16-ounce (475-ml) carton liquid egg whites

½ cup (115 g) low-fat or full-fat cottage cheese

2 whole eggs

½ teaspoon salt

¼ teaspoon pepper

½ teaspoon thyme

1 teaspoon turmeric

2 tablespoons (30 g) pesto

9 slices uncured Canadian bacon, diced

1 cup (70 g) desired veggies, chopped

¼ cup (38 g) crumbled feta or desired cheese, to top

Preheat oven to 350°F (180°C, or gas mark 4) and spray or line a 12-count muffin tin. I used silicone liners sprayed with avocado oil. Set aside.

In a large bowl pour egg whites, cottage cheese, whole eggs, spices, pesto, Canadian bacon, and veggies.

Stir well and break yolks.

Using a ⅓ cup measuring cup (40 ml), ladle mixture to fill muffin tin. Add desired cheese to top.

Bake for 20 to 25 minutes or until set. I put a cookie sheet under the muffin tin in case of spillage.

Per muffin   73 calories • 3 g fat • 4 g carbs • 1 g fiber • 9 g protein

Nourishment Breakdown

PROTEIN egg whites, cottage cheese, Canadian bacon	FAT cheese, yolks FIBER veggies	CARB/STARCH none

Vegan Protein Scramble

This one is perfect if you're egg-free and want an alternative source of protein. Make it for breakfast and even dinner. Leftovers are best heated in a warm skillet. If you want to add a carb/starch include a piece of toast or fruit.

14-ounce (400-g) block of firm tofu (organic is preferred)

½ cup (80 g) desired veggies (onion and spinach are favorites because they are easily frozen when low on groceries)

½ teaspoon turmeric

½ teaspoon garlic powder

¼ teaspoon salt

¼ teaspoon pepper

¼ teaspoon thyme

2 tablespoons (21 g) nutritional yeast

¼ cup (60 ml) almond milk

Drain the tofu. Layer a few paper towels and place the tofu on top, then weigh it down with a heavy book, or a large plate weighed down by a few canned goods from the pantry. Press the tofu for 15 minutes.

In a sprayed skillet over medium heat, add desired veggies and cook until fragrant and softened.

Next crumble the tofu with your hands into chunks and add to the pan. Season with all the seasonings, yeast, and add the milk.

Fry tofu until browned on the edges, usually about 5 to 6 minutes. Don't move around with the spatula as much as regular eggs so it keeps its shape.

Per serving 232 calories • 10 g fat • 11 g carbs • 4 g fiber • 22 g protein

Nourishment Breakdown

PROTEIN tofu, yeast

FAT tofu

FIBER veggies, yeast

CARB/STARCH none

Breakfast Meatballs

You can eat these protein-rich meatballs for blood sugar balance for breakfast or dinner. Make them ahead of time and add a piece of fruit or berries to go with them if you want a carb. Perfect for Christmas morning, and they even freeze well.

1 pound (450 g) ground chicken, 93% lean

1 pound (450 g) ground turkey breakfast sausage

½ Granny Smith apple, grated

½ yellow onion, diced

1 egg

¼ cup (23 g) coconut flour

¼ teaspoon sage

¼ teaspoon thyme

½ teaspoon salt

¼ teaspoon pepper

In a large bowl combine all ingredients with your hands. I used a cheese grater to grate the apple.

On a lined or sprayed sheet pan, use a ¼ cup (75 g) measuring scoop to form meatballs and place on the pan.

Bake at 350°F (180°C, or gas mark 4) for 25 to 30 minutes. Turn the oven to high broil and broil 2 to 3 minutes or until browned. Make sure the internal temperature is 175°F (80°C) and cooked through.

Per serving of 3 meatballs

366 calories • 21 g fat • 6 g carbs • 3 g fiber • 39 g protein

Nourishment Breakdown

PROTEIN chicken, turkey
FAT chicken, turkey

FIBER coconut flour, onion

CARB/STARCH small amount in apple

French Toast Protein Dip

I love Ezekiel bread which is a good protein source from the freezer section but use what you prefer. Gluten-free, low-carb/keto, or whole wheat breads all can work well. If using frozen Ezekiel, thaw slices ahead of time. You can do meal prep ahead of time and store it in the refrigerator.

1 egg

½ teaspoon cinnamon, divided

1 ounce (16 g) vanilla protein powder, divided

1 slice desired bread

½ cup (115 g) plain Greek yogurt

½ teaspoon vanilla extract

FRENCH TOAST

Add the egg to a small dish and whisk. Add ¼ teaspoon cinnamon and 1 tablespoon (8 g) protein powder. Whisk until the powder is incorporated into the egg.

Dip one slice of bread into egg wash on both sides and cook in a skillet over medium heat. Pour all egg mixture onto toast if there's any left.

After a few minutes, flip toast to cook the other side. Also, can be cooked in an air fryer at 350°F (180°C) for 3 to 5 minutes.

PROTEIN DIP

In a small bowl, add yogurt, vanilla extract, remaining ¼ teaspoon cinnamon, and remaining 1 tablespoon (8 g) protein powder. Stir well. Slice toast into 4 strips for dipping into yogurt and enjoy!

Per serving with nonfat yogurt and Ezekiel toast

330 calories • 6 g fat • 22 g carbs • 3 g fiber • 45 g protein

Nourishment Breakdown

PROTEIN powder, egg, yogurt

FAT egg yolk

FIBER some in bread

CARB/STARCH bread

The Blood Sugar Balance Cookbook

38

Turmeric Veggie Scramble

Eggs are always a simple, real-food, quick, anytime meal to throw together. I use them for breakfast, lunch, and dinner on those busy nights at the end of the week when groceries are low, and the kids eat out or eat "kid food." You can change flavors by choosing different cheeses and veggies. My favorites are Parmesan or crumbled goat cheese, and I've even used frozen veggies, cooking them in the microwave beforehand. All of these nutrients help to keep your blood sugar balanced.

1 cup (70 g) desired
   chopped vegetables

2 eggs

½ cup (120 ml) liquid egg whites
   or ½ cup (115 g) low-fat
   cottage cheese

½ teaspoon turmeric

¼ teaspoon pepper

¼ teaspoon salt

¼ teaspoon thyme

¼ cup (30 g) desired cheese

In a large, sprayed skillet over medium heat, add veggies to the pan and cook until softened.

Add the eggs and whites or cottage cheese. Add seasonings and stir with spatula to make a scramble. Adding cottage cheese will take a little longer to cook but makes them super creamy.

Once cooked to desired texture, add desired cheese to the top and enjoy!

Per serving with egg whites

343 calories • 16 g fat • 8 g carbs • 4 g fiber • 34 g protein

Per serving with low-fat cottage cheese

380 calories • 18 g fat • 15 g carbs • 4 g fiber • 34 g protein

Nourishment Breakdown

PROTEIN eggs, whites
cottage cheese
FAT yolks, cheese

FIBER vegetables
CARB/STARCH none, add a piece of
fruit or toast if desired.

Quick Mug Frittata

I love this as a quick savory breakfast or an anytime real-food meal to keep blood sugar stable. Guys, add another egg or more whites/cottage cheese if you'd like more protein and add a longer cooking time. You can't mess it up! Delicious with pickled onions when I have them on hand. Super easy to change out flavors with different veggies and cheese.

2 eggs

½ cup (120 ml) liquid egg whites or ½ cup (115 g) low-fat cottage cheese

3 tablespoons (36 g) green onion or spinach

2 tablespoons (10 g) grated Parmesan

¼ teaspoon salt

Dash pepper, sage, or thyme

Spray a mug with avocado or olive oil and set aside.

In a cereal bowl, add all ingredients and whisk to combine.

Microwave for 30 seconds; remove and stir.

Cook for another 30 seconds and stir again. Then cook 1 minute longer or until eggs are set.

OVEN DIRECTIONS

Cook at 350°F (180°C, or gas mark 4) for 20 minutes or until eggs are set as desired.

Per serving with whites

243 calories • 12 g fat • 1 g carbs • 30 g protein

Per serving with low-fat cottage cheese

260 calories • 14 g fat • 3 g carbs • 30 g protein

Nourishment Breakdown

PROTEIN eggs, whites/cottage cheese

FAT yolks, cheese

FIBER veggies

CARB/STARCH none, add toast or fruit if desired.

Balanced Chia Pudding

Protein, healthy fat, and fiber are the most important nutrients for balancing hunger hormones and blood sugar. This meal packs all those in a big way. It's a favorite that can be prepped in minutes and is yummy cold from the fridge and on the go. It has a similar texture to oatmeal but without grains. Chia seeds are rich in antioxidants, omega-3 fatty acids (helps raise HDL good cholesterol), iron, and calcium. Get creative with flavor variations! Some of my favorites are vanilla protein with berries and chocolate protein with banana for chunky monkey flavor.

1½ cups (355 ml) unsweetened milk of choice

1 banana or ⅔ cup (100 g) blueberries or any desired fruit, fresh or frozen

2 ounces (32 g) flavored protein powder

1 teaspoon salt

½ cup (88 g) chia seeds, divided

In a blender, add milk, desired fruit, protein powder, and salt. Blend well.

In 2 jars or covered dishes, add ¼ cup (44 g) chia seeds to each container.

Pour half of the blended mixture over the chia seeds and shake or store well.

Place in the fridge for 6 hours or overnight to allow the pudding to thicken. Store in the refrigerator. Good for a week.

Per serving with a banana
360 calories • 18 g fat • 40 g carbs • 25 g fiber • 32 g protein

Per serving with blueberries
327 calories • 18 g fat • 33 g carbs • 24 g fiber • 32 g protein

Nourishment Breakdown

PROTEIN powder   FIBER chia seeds
FAT chia seeds   CARB/STARCH banana

Balanced Yogurt Bowl

If you're going dairy-free or vegan, use an unsweetened coconut yogurt and a full serving of plant-based flavored collagen, or beef protein powder. If using plant-based protein powder, you may need to add a little water/milk if it's too thick. Also skip the other fat sources if your plant yogurt is high in fat. Most yogurt bowls are missing the fiber so they don't stabilize the hunger hormones, but this one will keep you feeling satisfied for hours.

¾ cup (180 g) nonfat plain Greek yogurt (if full-fat, skip the nuts for that just-right fat balance)

1 ounce (16 g) flavored protein powder

2 tablespoons (14 g) ground flaxseed, whole psyllium husk, or 1 tablespoon (15 g) psyllium husk powder

2 tablespoons (220 g) sliced almonds, peanuts, or (32 g) nut butter of choice

2 to 3 drops almond or vanilla extract, if desired

⅓ cup (57 g) desired fresh or frozen fruit

Add all ingredients to a small bowl and stir well.

Per serving, with 1 tablespoon husk, strawberries, and
2 tablespoons (220 g) sliced almonds

290 calories • 8 g fat • 22 g carbs • 8 g fiber • 33 g protein

Nourishment Breakdown

PROTEIN yogurt, powder
FAT nuts or full-fat yogurt, chia/flax

FIBER husk/chia/flax
CARB/STARCH fruit

FLAVOR SWAPS

APPLE PIE vanilla protein, cooked apple in cinnamon

CHOCOLATE-COVERED STRAWBERRY chocolate protein, strawberries

CHUNKY MONKEY chocolate protein, ⅓ cup (50 g) banana, peanut or peanut butter for fat

BANANA CREAM PIE vanilla protein, ⅓ cup (50 g) banana

PUMPKIN SPICE vanilla protein, ⅓ cup (82 g) pumpkin puree, add ½ teaspoon pumpkin pie spice, pumpkin seeds for fat

PINA COLADA vanilla protein, ⅓ cup (55 g) pineapple, unsweetened coconut flakes for fat

CORDIAL CHERRY chocolate protein, ⅓ cup (52 g) cherries

MOCHA chocolate protein, ⅓ cup (50 g) blueberries, add 2 teaspoons instant coffee

Breakfast

Smoked Salmon Protein Toast

1 SERVING

Make it for one or to feed company over the holidays. You can prep a whole container of cottage cheese with spices and have it ready to make the toast all week long. I love this one for a quick lunch to bring my blood sugar levels into balance at home too.

½ cup (115 g) low-fat or full-fat cottage cheese (dairy-free options below)

½ lemon, juiced

1 teaspoon fresh dill, chopped

1 slice desired bread, toasted

3 ounces (84 g) smoked salmon, thinly sliced (try to get wild-caught if it's available)

Dash salt and pepper or 'Everything but the Bagel' seasoning

OPTIONAL TOPPINGS

Raw or pickled red onion, fresh chives, 1 tablespoon (8 g) capers, handful arugula, 1 fried egg

Add cottage cheese, lemon juice, and dill to a small bowl and stir until combined. If you don't love the texture of cottage cheese, try blending a whole container and pouring it back into the container for easy storage.

Place mixture on a slice of toast. Add salmon, seasoning, and other toppings if desired.

Per serving without egg
280 calories • 6 g fat • 23 g carbs • 3 g fiber • 36 g protein

Per serving with egg
350 calories • 11 g fat • 23 g carbs • 3 g fiber • 42 g protein

Nourishment Breakdown

PROTEIN cottage cheese, salmon, egg	FAT egg, salmon, cottage cheese if full-fat	FIBER veggies, some in bread CARB/STARCH bread

NOTE *Dairy-free cottage cheese swap is dairy-free yogurt or 2 tablespoons (30 g) dairy-free cream cheese*

Basic Overnight N'Oatmeal

This recipe is easy to prep, and you can eat it anytime. N'Oats are perfect for my friends whose tummies don't do oats well or want to stay lower carb/keto. It's almost a whole day's worth of fiber and is high in protein, so it's a perfect breakfast meal to keep blood glucose in line and reduce late afternoon cravings. It's grain-free, dairy-free, and sugar-free.

1 cup (235 ml) milk of choice, unsweetened almond, cashew, or coconut

¼ cup (23 g) coconut flour

2 tablespoons (14 g) ground flaxseed or psyllium husk (whole flakes, 1 tablespoon [15 g] if using powder)

1 ounce (16 g) chocolate or vanilla flavored protein powder

1 ounce (20 g) collagen, optional

¼ teaspoon vanilla extract, optional

2 tablespoons (32 g) peanut butter

Add milk to a mason jar or a bowl with a cover. Add other ingredients, except the nut butter.

Stir well or shake well with lid on. Top with nut butter.

Store in the fridge. Good for a week.

Per serving with husk and 2 tablespoons peanut butter

494 calories • 19 g fat • 33 g carbs • 22 g fiber • 40 g protein

Nourishment Breakdown

PROTEIN powder	**FIBER** coconut flour,	**CARB/STARCH** none
FAT peanut butter, flax	seeds or husk	or jam/fruit if you want.

FLAVOR SWAPS

SUGAR COOKIE (vanilla protein), 2 drops vanilla or almond extract, 1 tablespoon (14 g) butter (fat)

ALMOND JOY (chocolate protein), 2 drops almond extract, 1 tablespoon (5 g) unsweetened coconut (fat)

REESE'S (chocolate protein), 1 tablespoon (16 g) peanut butter (fat)

GINGER SNAP (vanilla protein), ½ teaspoon molasses, ¼ teaspoon each ginger and all spice

CARROT CAKE (vanilla protein), ½ teaspoon cinnamon, ¼ teaspoon ginger, 2 tablespoons (14 g) shredded carrot

PUMPKIN SPICE (vanilla protein), ½ teaspoon pumpkin pie spice, 2 tablespoons (20 g) pumpkin seeds (fat)

MOCHA (chocolate protein), swap milk with coffee

SAVORY (unflavored protein powder), ½ teaspoon everything but the bagel seasoning or just salt and pepper, 1 tablespoon (14 g) grass-fed butter, melted, and a fried egg on top or ½ avocado (fat)

Basic Overnight Oatmeal

Easy breakfast prep that's loaded with all the nutrients including protein, healthy fats, and fiber for optimal blood sugar balance. There are eight different quick flavor swaps if you're like me and don't want the same flavor every single day. There's even a savory oats recipe for my savory fans. These are perfect if you're trying to up your fiber content too. Yummy cold on the go or heated up for a quick meal. For dairy-free, omit the yogurt and add more protein if you'd like. If you want to skip the oats, look for my N'Oatmeal recipe on page 47.

⅔ cup (160 ml) milk of choice unsweetened almond, cashew, or coconut

¼ cup (39 g) old-fashioned oats

2 tablespoons (24 g) flaxseeds, chia seeds, or whole psyllium husk (1 tablespoon [15 g] husk powder)

1 ounce (16 g) flavored protein powder

⅓ cup (77 g) nonfat plain Greek yogurt

1 tablespoon (16 g) desired nut butter

Add ingredients to a jar and shake or stir well.

Top with your favorite nut butter or unsweetened coconut flakes for healthy fats.

Let sit overnight to thicken. Good in the fridge for up to a week.

Per serving without toppings
300 calories • 5 g fat • 26 g carbs • 10 g fiber • 35 g protein

Per serving with 1 tablespoon peanut butter
380 calories • 13 g fat • 29 g carbs • 12 g fiber • 39 g protein

Nourishment Breakdown

PROTEIN powder and yogurt

FAT chia/flax, optional nut butter

FIBER chia/flax/husk

CARB/STARCH oats

FLAVOR SWAPS

SUGAR COOKIE (vanilla flavored protein), 2 drops vanilla or almond extract, 1 tablespoon (14 g) butter (fat)

ALMOND JOY (chocolate flavored protein), 2 drops almond extract, 1 tablespoon (5 g) unsweetened coconut (fat)

REESE'S (chocolate protein), 1 tablespoon (16 g) peanut butter (fat)

GINGER SNAP (vanilla protein), ½ teaspoon molasses, ¼ teaspoon each ginger and all spice

CARROT CAKE (vanilla protein), ½ teaspoon cinnamon, ¼ teaspoon ginger, 2 tablespoon (14 g) shredded carrot

PUMPKIN SPICE (vanilla protein), ½ teaspoon pumpkin pie spice, 2 tablespoons (20 g) pumpkin seeds (fat)

MOCHA (chocolate protein), Swap milk with coffee

SAVORY (unflavored protein powder), ½ teaspoon everything but the bagel seasoning or just salt and pepper, 1 tablespoon (14 g) grass-fed butter, melted and a fried egg on top or ½ avocado (fat)

Warm Peanut Butter & Jelly Protein Bowl

You'll love this one if you crave a warm cozy bowl of oatmeal with fruit on top like I do, but don't want a sugar spike. This recipe satisfies the oatmeal craving with two servings of veggies and half your day's worth of fiber. Grass-fed butter or sunflower butter is a great healthy fat swap if you go nut-free. You can cook frozen fruit with the cauliflower to make prep easier.

¼ cup (60 ml) milk of choice (I used unsweetened cashew)

1½ cup (161 g) frozen riced cauliflower

Dash pink salt

1 ounce (16 g) vanilla protein

1 ounce (20 g) collagen or more flavored protein to get to 30 g

2 tablespoons (14 g) ground flaxseed or whole psyllium husk, or 1 tablespoon (15 g) psyllium husk powder

⅓ cup (57 g) fresh berries of choice

2 tablespoons (32 g) natural peanut butter or 2 table-spoons (18 g) peanuts for a crunch

More salt to top

MICROWAVE

In a glass bowl add the milk, cauliflower, and salt. Cover with a paper towel.

Microwave 5 to 6 minutes. The key to not tasting the cauliflower is that it's cooked well.

Remove and add protein/collagen and flax/husk. Stir well and add more milk if desired or needed.

Add desired berries, peanut butter, and a little more salt if desired.

STOVETOP

In a skillet or saucepan, add milk, cauliflower, and salt.

Cook over medium heat covered until cauliflower is softened.

Remove from heat and add protein/collagen and flax/husk. Pour in a bowl and add desired berries, peanut butter, and more salt if desired.

Per serving
340 calories • 15 g fat • 22 g carbs • 13 g fiber • 40 g protein

Nourishment Breakdown

PROTEIN powder	**FIBER** flax, husk, cauliflower
FAT peanut butter, flax if using	**CARB/STARCH** berries

Almond Joy Warm Protein Bowl

This is like a big, warm bowl of oatmeal that will keep blood sugar levels stable. You might be skeptical about cauliflower but if you cook it long enough, it has a very mild taste. If you'd like, add a carb, top it with ⅓ cup (48 g) of berries, mash in half of a banana, or enjoy a piece of fruit on the side.

¼ cup (60 ml) milk of choice (I used unsweetened cashew)

1½ cup (161 g) frozen riced cauliflower (or a little more)

¼ teaspoon coconut or almond extract, optional

¼ cup (20 g) unsweetened coconut flakes

½ teaspoon pink salt

1 ounce (16 g) chocolate protein powder

1 ounce (20 g) collagen, or flavored protein powder to get to 30 g protein

1 tablespoon (5 g) cacao or unsweetened cocoa powder, optional extra chocolate

2 tablespoons (14 g) ground flaxseed, whole psyllium husk (or 1 tablespoon [15 g] psyllium husk powder)

1 tablespoon (11 g) cacao nibs or dark chocolate chips as a topping

More salt or flake sea salt, optional

More coconut flakes, optional

MICROWAVE

In a glass bowl add the milk, cauliflower, extract, coconut, and salt.

Cover with a paper towel. Microwave 6 minutes. The key to not tasting the cauliflower is to cook it well done.

Add protein/collagen, optional cacao/cocoa powder, and flax/husk. Stir well and add more milk if desired/needed. Top with chocolate, salt if desired, and a sprinkle of more coconut.

STOVETOP

In a skillet or saucepan, add milk, cauliflower, extract, coconut, and salt.

Cook over medium heat covered until cauliflower is softened and cooked.

Remove from heat and add protein/collagen, cocoa powder, and flax/husk. Pour in a bowl and top with chocolate, more salt, and/or coconut if desired, and a splash of more milk.

Per serving with husk, ¼ cup (20 g) coconut, and 1 tablespoon (11 g) stevia-sweetened dark chips

380 calories • 13 g fat • 25 g carbs • 18 g fiber • 34 g protein

Nourishment Breakdown

PROTEIN powder
FAT coconut, dark chips, flax

FIBER flax, husk, cauliflower
CARB/STARCH none

Sweet Potato Protein Bowl

If you're a fan of sweet potato casserole, you'll enjoy this taste of Thanksgiving that you can have all year long. The vitamin A in sweet potatoes is fat-soluble and easily absorbed. It's also vital for a healthy liver, immune system, heart, kidneys, and thyroid function, and this is a yummy way to get what you need. If you're nut-free or not a fan of nut butter, 1 tablespoon (14 g) of grass-fed butter or unsweetened coconut will work great too. Keep in mind that cooked carbs, like potatoes and rice, can keep blood sugar levels more stable and have prebiotic gut benefits. Cooking several potatoes as a prep and storing in the fridge can be helpful for gut health and an effective blood sugar hack too.

1 medium (fist-size) sweet potato, cooked or ½ cup (123 g) canned

¼ cup (60 ml) milk of choice

1 ounce (16 g) vanilla protein powder

1 ounce (20 g) collagen, or more protein powder to get to 30 g

1 tablespoon (7 g) ground flaxseed or psyllium husk

1 teaspoon cinnamon or pumpkin pie spice

1 tablespoon (16 g) peanut butter

OPTIONAL TOPPINGS

2 tablespoons (14 g) low-sugar granola

2 tablespoons (10 g) unsweetened coconut flakes

Remove skin and mash potato with a fork (microwave or heat on the stovetop to reheat if it's cold from storing in the fridge).

Add all other ingredients except nut butter and stir.

Top with your favorite nut butter for your healthy fat source. Sometimes I add a little granola and unsweetened coconut to give it that sweet potato casserole topping feel.

Per serving with 1 tablespoon peanut butter

360 calories • 9 g fat • 31 g carbs • 7 g fiber • 34 g protein

Nourishment Breakdown

PROTEIN powder
FAT flax if using, nut butter, coconut, granola

FIBER husk/flax
CARB/STARCH sweet potato

Sugar Cookie Warm Protein Bowl

This one is a favorite of mine when I'm craving comfort food for breakfast on a chilly day. It's high in fiber and low in carbs and will keep you in the right blood sugar zone.

¼ cup (60 ml) milk of choice (I used unsweetened cashew)

1½ cup (161 g) frozen riced cauliflower

¼ teaspoon cake batter, vanilla, or almond extract

1 tablespoon (14 g) grass-fed butter

½ mashed banana, optional

½ teaspoon pink salt

1 ounce (16 g) vanilla protein powder

1 ounce (20 g) collagen or another 1 ounce (16 g) flavored protein powder

2 tablespoons (14 g) ground flaxseed, whole psyllium husk, or 1 tablespoon (15 g) psyllium husk powder

Desired colorful sprinkles, optional

MICROWAVE

In a glass bowl add the milk, cauliflower, extract, butter, banana if desired, and salt.

Cover with a paper towel. Microwave 6 minutes. The key to not tasting the cauliflower is to cook it well done.

Remove and add protein and flax/husk. Stir well and add more milk if desired/needed. Add sprinkles if using.

STOVETOP

In a skillet or saucepan, add milk, cauliflower, extract, butter, banana if desired, and salt.

Cook over medium heat covered until cauliflower is softened and cooked.

Remove from heat and add protein/collagen and flax/husk. Pour in a bowl and add a splash of more milk, if needed/desired. Add sprinkles if using.

Per serving with husk and banana

372 calories • 13 g fat • 29 g carbs • 13 g fiber • 32 g protein

Per serving without banana

322 calories • 13 g fat • 16 g carbs • 11 g fiber • 32 g protein

Nourishment Breakdown

PROTEIN powder
FAT butter, flax

FIBER cauliflower, husk/flax
CARB/STARCH banana or none

Cottage Cheese Bowls

Who doesn't love a meat-free meal as a last-minute option? Savory or sweet, this dish will satisfy whatever you're craving that day. It makes a no-cook quick balanced meal and curbs overeating.

SWEET BOWL

1 cup (225 g) low-fat or full-fat cottage cheese

1 peach or ⅓ cup (57 g) of any desired fruit

¼ cup (27 g) low-sugar granola

1 tablespoon (5 g) unsweetened coconut flakes

Dash cinnamon or pumpkin pie spice

SAVORY BOWL

1 cup (225 g) low-fat or full-fat cottage cheese

1 small or ½ large cooked potato (I cooked a whole bag of organic ones and keep in the fridge)

¼ teaspoon everything but the bagel seasoning

Desired hot sauce or hummus

Desired pickles, optional

Desired pickled onions, optional

NOTE *You can skip the potato and use any veggie you'd like; tomatoes and cucumbers are a popular savory option.*

Place cottage cheese in a bowl. Add all other ingredients and enjoy!

The amount of cottage cheese depends on hunger. For a snack, ½ cup (115 g) is great. For a meal, 1 cup (225 g) gives you 30 g of protein.

Per serving of sweet bowl

395 calories • 18 g fat • 30 g carbs • 4 g fiber • 33 g protein

Nourishment Breakdown

PROTEIN cottage cheese
FAT granola, coconut, cottage cheese if full fat

FIBER some in fruit
CARB/STARCH fruit

Per serving of savory bowl with medium potato and hummus

321 calories • 5 g fat • 43 g carbs • 4 g fiber • 30 g protein

Nourishment Breakdown

PROTEIN cottage cheese
FAT not much unless using full-fat cottage cheese

FIBER some in potato, pickles, onions
CARB/STARCH potato

Balanced Breakfast Casserole (Mediterranean Flavor)

I make this when we do a breakfast-for-dinner night. It's also on our Christmas morning and Easter brunch menu every year. This recipe is perfect because it contains no carbs, just protein and fiber to counterbalance the simple sugars of traditional cinnamon rolls, pastries, or that chocolate Santa or Easter Bunny. The flavor swaps are fun for a seasonal change up.

1 pound (450 g) turkey ground breakfast sausage

10 ounces (190 g) grape tomatoes, sliced in half

1 cup (30 g) spinach or (67 g) kale, chopped

16-ounce (475-ml) carton egg whites

6 whole eggs

1 teaspoon basil

1 teaspoon salt

1 teaspoon pepper

⅓ cup (50 g) crumbled feta cheese

In a heated skillet over medium heat, brown sausage and crumble. Add veggies and cook for 5 minutes to soften.

Add egg whites and whole eggs to a bowl. Add seasonings to eggs and whisk.

Add meat and veggie mixture to a 9 x 13-inch (23 x 33-cm) glass dish. Pour egg mixture over meat and top with cheese.

Bake at 400°F (200°C, or gas mark 6) for 15 minutes or until set. Switch the oven to broil on high for 1 minute or so to brown the top if desired. Watch it because it burns quickly. You can also make ahead of time, store in the fridge uncooked and covered, and bake before enjoying.

(see next page for flavor swaps)

Per serving   278 calories • 16 g fat • 2 g carbs • 28 g protein

Nourishment Breakdown

PROTEIN eggs, whites, sausage	FIBER all the veggies	CARB/STARCH none, so perfect for holiday
FAT sausage, yolks, cheese		cinnamon rolls or biscuits, toast, or fruit

BALANCED BREAKFAST CASSEROLE FLAVOR SWAPS

(using the same eggs, whites, and sausage as listed in main recipe on page 55)

CLASSIC VEGGIE 1 onion, chopped, 8 ounces (72 g) mushrooms, chopped, 10 ounces (190 g) grape tomatoes, cut in half, 12 ounces (234 g) broccoli, chopped, 1 teaspoon thyme, 1 teaspoon garlic powder, 1 teaspoon each salt and pepper, ⅓ cup (38 g) aged cheddar, shredded

FALL 1 apple, chopped, 1 onion, chopped, 1 teaspoon thyme, 1 teaspoon sage, 1 teaspoon garlic powder, ½ teaspoon nutmeg, 1 teaspoon each salt and pepper, ⅓ cup (50 g) goat cheese

MEXICAN 10 ounces (225 g) tomatoes with green chilis, drained, 1 tablespoon (7 g) taco seasoning, 1 teaspoon each salt and pepper, ⅓ cup (38 g) Cotija or cheddar cheese, top with salsa

SOUTHERN 1 pound (56 g) country uncured ham, diced (instead of sausage), 4 ounces (60 g) green chilies, chopped, 1 onion, chopped, 1 tablespoon (11 g) Dijon mustard, 1 teaspoon pepper, ⅓ cup (38 g) cheddar, shredded

Shown: Balanced Breakfast Casserole, Mediterranean Flavor, page 55

5

Smoothies

WHETHER IT'S A MEAL or a snack, smoothies are a convenient way to consume important blood sugar balancing nutrients at once, especially if you're on the go. Some of these recipes include veggies like zucchini, yellow squash, or frozen cauliflower, which can be cooked or steamed before freezing or frozen raw. Since the protein powder you choose will be the main flavor when it comes to smoothies, try a few until you find one that you really enjoy. Or rotate several types to add variety.

Strawberry Matcha Smoothie

This is a great pick-me-up and balanced sweet-tooth fix in one. There's 40 to 50 mg of caffeine in this smoothie from the matcha, so if you're sensitive to its effects, don't have this one too late in the day. Matcha is rich in catechins, a type of plant compounds in tea that act as natural antioxidants. Matcha smoothie cheers!

1 cup (235 ml) milk of choice
(I used unsweetened cashew)

2 teaspoons matcha powder, culinary grade

2 tablespoons (32 g) peanut or almond butter

⅓ cup (48 g) strawberries, fresh or frozen

1 tablespoon (12 g) flaxseed, chia seeds, or psyllium husk (used 1 tablespoon [15 g] husk powder)

½ teaspoon vanilla extract

1 ounce (16 g) vanilla flavored protein powder

1 ounce (20 g) vanilla, unflavored collagen, or ½ cup (115 g) nonfat Greek yogurt

1 cup (240 g) ice

1 cup (30 g) spinach, fresh or frozen

Dash pink salt

Add ingredients in the order listed to the blender and blend well.

Per serving with unsweetened cashew milk and 1 tablespoon (15 g) psyllium husk

443 calories • 15 g fat • 26 g carbs • 15 g fiber • 40 g protein

Nourishment Breakdown

PROTEIN powder, yogurt	FIBER spinach, husk/flax/chia
FAT nut butter, chia/flax	CARB/STARCH strawberries

Peanut Butter Mocha Cheesecake Smoothie

This is a favorite if you need a quick pick-me-up, thanks to the caffeine it contains, but the protein and fats help prevent a sugar spike. If you aren't a coffee or mocha fan, swap the coffee for more milk and you've got a chocolate peanut butter cheesecake smoothie which is just as delicious.

½ cup (120 ml) cold brew or leftover coffee

½ cup (120 ml) unsweetened almond or cashew milk

2 tablespoons (32 g) natural peanut butter (I put 1 tablespoon in the smoothie and 1 tablespoon on top)

½ cup (115 g) low-fat cottage cheese (if full-fat, do 1 tablespoon [16 g] peanut butter for fat balance)

1 ounce (16 g) chocolate protein powder

1 cup (107 g) frozen riced cauliflower or (120 g) frozen yellow squash

¼ teaspoon pink salt

Add ingredients in the order listed to the blender and blend well.

For dairy-free, swap cottage cheese with unsweetened plant-based yogurt and use a full serving of protein powder. You may need to use less peanut butter if your yogurt is high in fat.

Per serving with 1 tablespoon (8 g) protein powder

420 calories • 18 g fat • 13 g carbs • 5 g fiber • 38 g protein

Nourishment Breakdown

PROTEIN cottage cheese, powder
FAT nut butter

FIBER veggies
CARB/STARCH none

Lemon Bar Smoothie

A delicious snack that will satisfy your hunger without the spike. The turmeric in this recipe is a bonus because of its antioxidant and anti-inflammatory properties. A simple and highly effective way of increasing turmeric absorption is to add a pinch of pepper and a fat source. Together, the ingredients make a tasty and balancing snack.

1 cup (235 ml) milk of choice
(I used unsweetened cashew)

2 tablespoons (32 g) cashew or almond butter (¼ cup [34 g] whole cashews works too)

1 lemon, juiced

1 tablespoon (6 g) lemon rind

1 tablespoon (7 g) flaxseed, psyllium husk (I used 1 tablespoon [15 g] husk powder)

½ teaspoon vanilla extract

1 ounce (16 g) vanilla flavored protein powder

1 ounce (20 g) vanilla or unflavored collagen

1 cup (240 g) ice

½ cup (54 g) frozen cauliflower, whole or riced

Dash pink salt

½ teaspoon turmeric

Dash pepper (to activate turmeric)

Low-sugar granola, optional

Add ingredients in the order listed to the blender and blend well.

I top with a low-sugar granola for a "crust" taste. Low sugar is usually considered 5 g of sugar or less per serving. That's what I look for at the grocery store.

Per serving with 1 tablespoon husk

406 calories • 17 g fat • 19 g carbs • 14 g fiber • 42 g protein

Nourishment Breakdown

PROTEIN powder
FAT nuts, granola if adding, flax
FIBER cauliflower, husk/flax

CARB/STARCH small amount in lemon juice

Basic Vanilla Smoothie

A classic smoothie. I love that this one is fruit-free. But you can enjoy it as a low-carb meal or have a piece of fruit on the side, especially if using as a post-workout meal. This smoothie helps replenish glucose stores in your muscles so that this energy source is available when you need it.

1 cup (235 ml) milk of choice
   (I used unsweetened cashew)

2 tablespoons (32 g) cashew or
   almond butter (½ avocado
   works too)

1 tablespoon (7 g) flaxseed,
   psyllium husk (used 1 tablespoon [15 g] husk powder)

½ teaspoon vanilla extract

1 ounce (16 g) vanilla flavored
   protein powder

1 ounce (20 g) vanilla or
   unflavored collagen

1 cup (240 g) ice or (120 g)
   frozen yellow squash/
   cauliflower

½ cup (15 g) spinach, optional

Dash pink salt

Add ingredients in the order listed to the blender and blend well.

Per serving   425 calories • 17 g fat • 16 g carbs • 12 g fiber • 40 g protein

Nourishment Breakdown

PROTEIN powder
FAT nut butter/avocado, flax
FIBER husk/flax

CARB/STARCH none, add a piece of
fruit to the side, if desired

Sleepy Dinnertime Smoothie

This smoothie is packed with all kinds of nutrients that nourish the body and help you sleep well. When you do, blood sugar regulation is easier. Flaxseeds, for example, are rich in omega-3 fatty acids, which help reduce stress, anxiety, and inflammation. Cherries contain vitamins A and C along with magnesium and melatonin, which aid relaxation and sleep. Almonds contain magnesium and melatonin as well. Chamomile tea contains the flavonoid known as apigenin, which binds to receptors in the brain that may help someone become sleepy. Cheers and sweet dreams!

1 cup (235 ml) milk of choice (I used unsweetened cashew) or brewed chamomile tea

2 tablespoons (32 g) almond butter

⅓ cup (52 g) pitted cherries, fresh or frozen

1 tablespoon (7 g) flaxseed

1 ounce (16 g) vanilla or chocolate flavored protein powder

1 ounce (20 g) collagen

1 cup (240 g) ice

Dash pink salt

¼ teaspoon nutmeg

½ teaspoon cinnamon

Add ingredients in the order listed to the blender and blend well.

Per serving 424 calories • 20 g fat • 15 g carbs • 7 g fiber • 39 g protein

Nourishment Breakdown

PROTEIN powder
FAT almond butter, flax

FIBER flax
CARB/STARCH cherries

Glowing Skin Smoothie

This smoothie is full of vitamins, minerals, and antioxidants that can help improve your skin's health. Nutrients in plant-based foods such as vitamin C, vitamin E, beta-carotene, and polyphenols function as antioxidants which help reduce inflammation, promote the skin's structural support, and defend against oxidation. The protein and fiber from the veggies help even out blood sugar levels.

1 cup (235 ml) unsweetened milk of choice or brewed green tea (cooled)

1 ounce (16 g) vanilla or chocolate protein powder

1 ounce (20 g) collagen, optional

⅓ cup (58 g) mango, fresh or frozen

½ avocado, frozen

1 whole raw carrot, chopped

½ teaspoon cinnamon

½ teaspoon turmeric

¼ teaspoon pink salt

Dash pepper (to activate the turmeric)

1 cup (240 g) ice

2 tablespoons (22 g) cacao nibs, optional topping

Add ingredients, except cacao nibs, to the blender and blend well.

Top with nibs and enjoy.

Per serving   359 calories • 13 g fat • 26 g carbs • 12 g fiber • 35 g protein

Nourishment Breakdown

PROTEIN powder
FAT avocado, cacao nibs

FIBER carrot, avocado
CARB/STARCH mango

Pineapple Vanilla Cream Smoothie

This smoothie will remind you of summer treats any time of the year. Pineapples are nutrient rich in vitamins such as vitamin B6, folate, niacin, riboflavin, vitamin C, and minerals like manganese, copper, thiamin, potassium, magnesium, and iron. Pineapples are also high in fiber, which when combined with the protein and fat here, make this a well-rounded and blood sugar balanced smoothie.

1 cup (235 ml) milk of choice (I used unsweetened cashew)

1 tablespoon (16 g) cashew or almond butter (peanut butter works, too, you can just taste it)

½ cup (115 g) low-fat cottage cheese (if full fat, skip the nut butter for fat balance)

2 tablespoons (24 g) flaxseed, psyllium husk, or chia seeds (I used 2 tablespoons [30 g] husk)

½ teaspoon vanilla extract

1 ounce (16 g) vanilla flavored protein powder

⅓ cup (55 g) pineapple, fresh or frozen

1 cup (132 g) frozen cauliflower

Dash pink salt

Add ingredients in the order listed to the blender and blend well.

Per serving with 2 tablespoons (30 g) psyllium husk

350 calories • 11 g fat • 20 g carbs • 9 g fiber • 32 g protein

Nourishment Breakdown

PROTEIN cottage cheese, powder
FAT nut butter, flax/chia

FIBER husk/flax/chia
CARB/STARCH pineapple

NOTE *For dairy-free, swap cottage cheese with unsweetened plant-based yogurt and use a full serving of protein powder. You may need to use less nut butter if the yogurt you choose is high in fat.*

Almond Joy Smoothie

This is a yummy recipe that will satisfy any sweet tooth without affecting your blood sugar levels. Just be careful with your almond extract pour. It can be super strong and overwhelm the flavor.

1 cup (235 ml) milk of choice (I used unsweetened almond)

1 ounce (16 g) chocolate protein powder

1 tablespoon (15 g) psyllium husk or husk powder

¼ cup (20 g) frozen coconut chunks or unsweetened flakes

1 cup (240 g) ice or (120 g) frozen yellow squash/ zucchini

1 ounce (20 g) collagen or ½ ounce (8 g) more chocolate protein

¼ teaspoon almond extract

Dash pink salt

Low-sugar granola or coconut flakes, optional topping

Add ingredients in the order listed to the blender and blend well.

Add a sprinkle of low-sugar granola and/or coconut flakes if you want a crunchy topping. Serve with fruit on the side, if desired.

Per serving with 2 tablespoons (30 g) of husk

365 calories • 10 g fat • 19 g carbs • 11 g fiber • 33 g protein

Nourishment Breakdown

PROTEIN powder

FAT coconut

FIBER husk, squash/zucchini

CARB/STARCH none

Raspberries & Cream Smoothie

This is one of my favorites. You can use just about any berry which makes this a colorful and yummy smoothie. Thanks to the plant butter, protein, and fiber, you'll feel full and satisfied and your blood sugar will remain in balance.

1 cup (235 ml) unsweetened milk of choice

1 tablespoon (16 g) cashew or almond butter (peanut butter works, too, you can just taste it)

½ cup (115 g) low-fat cottage cheese (if full-fat, skip the nut butter for fat balance)

2 tablespoons (24 g) flaxseed, psyllium husk, or chia (I used 2 tablespoons [30 g] husk)

½ teaspoon vanilla extract

1 ounce (16 g) vanilla protein powder

⅓ cup (42 g) raspberries, fresh or frozen

1 cup (240 g) ice

Dash pink salt

Add ingredients in the order listed to the blender and blend well.

Per serving with 2 tablespoons (24 g) husk

341 calories • 11 g fat • 18 g carbs • 11 g fiber • 32 g protein

Nourishment Breakdown

PROTEIN cottage cheese, powder
FAT nut butter, flax/chia

FIBER husk/flax/chia
CARB/STARCH raspberries

NOTE *For dairy-free, swap cottage cheese with unsweetened plant-based yogurt and use a full serving of protein powder. You may need to use less nut butter if the yogurt you choose is high in fat.*

Chunky Monkey Smoothie

This one never gets old! Perfect for a post-workout meal to cool off and replenish your body. Keep in mind that after you exercise you have extra storage space in your muscles for the carbs found in this recipe. This means that glucose will be available when you need it later to keep blood sugar levels stable.

1 cup (235 ml) unsweetened almond milk

Dash pink salt

2 tablespoons (32 g) natural peanut butter (only peanuts and salt as ingredients)

1 ounce (16 g) chocolate protein

1 ounce (20 g) chocolate or unflavored collagen

1 tablespoon (5 g) unsweetened cacao powder, optional

1 cup (240 g) ice

1 tablespoon (15 g) whole psyllium husk (use 1 table-spoon [15 g] if husk powder)

½ frozen banana

1 tablespoon (11 g) cacao nibs, optional topping

Add all ingredients, except cacao nibs, in the order listed to the blender and blend well.

Topped here with cacao nibs for a crunch and that vital chewing so you're satisfied.

Per serving without toppings

460 calories • 15 g fat • 28 g carbs • 13 g fiber • 42 g protein

Nourishment Breakdown

PROTEIN powder
FAT peanut butter

FIBER husk
CARB/STARCH banana

Peanut Butter Cream Pie Smoothie

This smoothie is creamy and delicious. You won't find any carbs in this recipe so you can add a piece of fruit or toast on the side if you like. The protein and fats do the work here and will keep you feeling full, so you'll be less likely to crave sweets or overeat.

1 cup (235 ml) unsweetened almond or cashew milk

2 tablespoons (32 g) natural peanut butter

½ cup (115 g) low-fat cottage cheese (if full-fat, add 1 tablespoon [16 g] peanut butter for fat balance)

1 ounce (16 g) vanilla protein powder

1 cup (107 g) frozen riced cauliflower or (120 g) frozen yellow squash

¼ teaspoon pink salt

Add ingredients in the order listed to the blender and blend well.

Per serving with 1 tablespoon (8 g) protein powder

435 calories • 18 g fat • 15 g carbs • 5 g fiber • 38 g protein

Nourishment Breakdown

PROTEIN cottage cheese, powder
FAT nut butter

FIBER veggies
CARB/STARCH none

NOTE *For dairy-free, swap cottage cheese with unsweetened plant-based yogurt and use a full serving of protein powder. You may need to use less peanut butter if the yogurt you choose is high in fat. Check the label.*

Snickers Smoothie

I love crunchy peanuts and chocolate, so this one always satisfies. It also contains fiber to slow digestion and keep blood sugar levels stable. Make this protein-rich smoothie ahead of time and enjoy a nutrient-dense meal on the go.

1 cup (235 ml) unsweetened almond milk

1 date, pitted

Dash pink salt

2 tablespoons (18 g) salted peanuts, divided

1 ounce (16 g) chocolate protein

1 ounce (20 g) chocolate or unflavored collagen

1 tablespoon (5 g) unsweetened cacao powder, optional

1 cup (240 g) ice or (120 g) frozen zucchini/yellow squash

½ teaspoon vanilla extract

2 tablespoons (30 g) whole psyllium husk (1 tablespoon [15 g] husk powder)

Add milk and the date to the blender and blend well.

Add other ingredients in the order listed to the blender and blend well. I like to do 1 tablespoon (9 g) peanuts in smoothie and the other 1 tablespoon to top for a crunch.

Per serving   420 calories • 15 g fat • 20 g carbs • 11 g fiber • 42 g protein

Nourishment Breakdown

PROTEIN powder

FAT peanuts

FIBER husk

CARB/STARCH date

Cinnamon Toast Smoothie

This smoothie is as tasty as cinnamon toast but won't lead to a blood sugar spike. When I have an almost-empty jar of nut butter, I turn to this recipe and add what's left to the smoothie. Flaxseed acts as fiber and a fat and is also a blood sugar stabilizer.

1 cup (235 ml) milk of choice (I used unsweetened cashew)

2 tablespoons (32 g) cashew or almond butter (peanut butter works, too, you can just taste it)

2 tablespoons (14 g) flaxseed or psyllium husk (I used 1 tablespoon [15 g] husk powder)

½ teaspoon vanilla extract or butter extract

½ teaspoon cinnamon

1 ounce (16 g) vanilla flavored protein powder

1 cup (240 g) ice or (120 g) frozen yellow squash/ cauliflower

Dash pink salt

1 date, optional to sweeten

Add ingredients in the order listed to the blender and blend well. If using 2 tablespoons (14 g) ground flaxseed, use 1 tablespoon (16 g) of the nut butter to tweak your healthy fats. Flax is a fat and fiber source. Also, adding the date adds 20 calories and 5 g of carbs from sugar.

Per serving with 2 tablespoons (32 g) almond butter and
1 tablespoon (15 g) husk

410 calories • 17 g fat • 14 g carbs • 11 g fiber • 37 g protein

Nourishment Breakdown

PROTEIN powder
FAT nut butter, flax

FIBER husk/flax
CARB/STARCH none or date

6

Lunch

LUNCH IS IMPORTANT but often we get busy and skip it or spend the afternoon grazing and snacking on unhealthy options due to extreme hunger or low blood sugar levels. Eating a nutritious lunch helps control hunger and prevents overeating later in the day.

Remember, by lunchtime, your body has already used a significant amount of energy, and your blood sugar levels may have dropped since breakfast. So, lunch provides the necessary nutrients to refuel your body, providing energy for the remainder of the day.

Lunch can be social when you share a meal with a friend, family, or colleague. It also can be a much-needed break from work or your usual busy schedule. Stress affects blood sugar levels, so by taking the time to relax and eat a healthy lunch, you help to rest and replenish your body and yourself.

Balanced Meal Egg Salad

This recipe is super popular and easy to make. I often buy boiled eggs to simplify it even more. Most egg salad recipes are higher in fat because of the mayo and egg yolks. I've tweaked this recipe so that it has moderate fat and high protein to shut off hunger better and keep you satisfied until your next meal.

12 eggs, boiled

⅓ cup (77 g) nonfat Greek yogurt (plenty of fat in eggs, so I skip mayo on this one)

1 tablespoon (11 g) yellow mustard

1 tablespoon (15 ml) apple cider vinegar

4 green onions, chopped, optional

2 tablespoons (8 g) fresh dill or (30 g) dill relish

½ teaspoon each salt and pepper

Mash eggs with a pastry cutter.

Add all other ingredients and stir well. Store in the fridge. Good for a week.

Per serving   320 calories • 18 g fat • 3 g carbs • 30 g protein

Nourishment Breakdown

PROTEIN eggs, yogurt
FAT egg yolks

FIBER relish, onion
CARB/STARCH none

High-Protein Pimento Cheese

This is a high-protein twist on a southern classic recipe. I usually put it on a low-carb wrap or pita with salad greens, on a salad, on toast with melted pimento cheese, or with a pear or a serving of crackers as my starch. This makes for a quick, easy, balanced meal and an easy lunch.

2 cups (450 g) low-fat
  cottage cheese

3 tablespoons (36 g) pimentos

3 tablespoons (27 g) diced green
  chilies or jalapeños, optional

½ cup (115 g) nonfat or
  2% Greek yogurt

8 ounces (115 g) sharp cheddar,
  shredded

½ teaspoon garlic powder

Salt and pepper, to taste

Place ingredients in a bowl and stir well to combine. If you don't love the texture of cottage cheese, blend it first in the blender or food processor until smooth. Then add all other ingredients and stir.

Good for a week in the fridge. Great meal prep.

Per serving   150 calories • 8 g fat • 4 g carbs • 18 g protein

Nourishment Breakdown

PROTEIN cottage cheese, yogurt

FAT cheddar cheese

FIBER none

CARB/STARCH none

Carrot Cake Protein Toast

This recipe tastes good, will fill you up, and is good for your blood sugar. If you aren't a fan of the cottage cheese texture, put the cottage cheese mixture in a blender and blend first. For vegan swaps, use unsweetened coconut yogurt (instead of cottage cheese) and a full serving of vanilla protein powder. My go-to granolas for happy blood sugar are in the 5 g of sugar or less per serving range. There are usually several in this range at the grocery store.

1 slice cinnamon raisin toast (or regular works)
½ cup (115 g) low-fat cottage cheese
1 tablespoon (8 g) vanilla protein powder
1 tablespoon (7 g) chopped pecans or walnuts
½ teaspoon cinnamon
¼ teaspoon or a dash of each ginger and nutmeg
Top with granola, if desired for a crunch

Toast your bread.

In a bowl, combine remaining ingredients except the granola.

Place mixture on top of toast and sprinkle granola on top if desired.

Per serving without granola

290 calories • 8 g fat • 21 g carbs • 3 g fiber • 35 g protein

Nourishment Breakdown

PROTEIN cottage cheese, powder
FAT granola, nuts
FIBER some in bread
CARB/STARCH bread

Tuna Quesadilla

This recipe is an easy fix to keep your blood sugar in check. Often, I add veggies or a salad for fiber and fullness and a bit of dark chocolate for dessert. Keep in mind that the carb total can vary depending on the brand of tortillas.

2½ ounces (70 g) canned tuna or 2.5 ounces (70 g) canned salmon

2 teaspoons pesto

¼ teaspoon everything but the bagel seasoning, optional

1 low-carb or high-fiber tortilla

1 slice desired cheese (provolone and Swiss are my favorites)

Drain liquid from tuna or salmon and stir in pesto and seasoning. Spray avocado or olive oil in a skillet. Place tortilla, fish mixture, and cheese in skillet over medium heat.

Fold in half to cover and allow to heat until tortilla is browned. Spray the upper side of tortilla before you flip it. Cook on the other side and enjoy.

Per serving   310 calories • 11 g fat • 12 g carbs • 7 g fiber • 41 g protein

Nourishment Breakdown

PROTEIN tuna/salmon

FAT cheese, pesto

FIBER some in tortilla

CARB/STARCH tortilla

Savory Protein Veggie Dip

This is one of my favorite lunch recipes when I'm craving a savory meal. It's easy to prep ahead of time. Enjoy half the recipe and share the rest with a friend or use it as an appetizer to get more protein and fiber into your day to balance blood sugar. My favorite dipping veggies are broccoli, mini sweet peppers, radishes, raw whole carrots, and celery.

¾ cup (180 g) plain
    Greek yogurt
½ cup (115 g) low-fat
    cottage cheese
½ teaspoon everything but
    the bagel seasoning or
    1 teaspoon ranch seasoning
1 cup (70 g) desired veggies
    for dipping
Seeded crackers, optional

In a medium bowl, stir together yogurt, cottage cheese, and seasoning. You can also blend the cottage cheese first if you're not a fan of the texture.

Dip desired vegetables and crackers and enjoy.

Per serving with 12 seeded crackers and nonfat yogurt
410 calories • 95 g fat • 40 g carbs • 7 g fiber • 38 g protein

Per serving without crackers and nonfat yogurt
260 calories • 25 g fat • 23 g carbs • 4 g fiber • 33 g protein

Nourishment Breakdown
PROTEIN yogurt, cottage cheese
FAT cottage cheese
FIBER veggies
CARB/STARCH crackers

Brownie Protein Dip

This protein dip is one of my most popular recipes, so I knew I had to include one in this book. You can meal prep this one ahead of time in a covered dish for a meal or a larger snack to keep blood sugar in balance between meals. I often enjoy a few bites for dessert and put it back in the fridge to store for later. If you use full-fat yogurt, you can skip the almond butter to keep fat moderate and not high. If you're going nut-free, sunflower butter is a great healthy fat option.

⅔ cup (154 g) nonfat
    Greek yogurt

1 ounce (16 g) chocolate
    flavored protein powder

1 tablespoon (16 g) almond or
    cashew butter

¼ teaspoon vanilla extract

1 tablespoon (6 g) coconut flour,
    optional

1 tablespoon (11 g) dark
    chocolate chips

1 apple, sliced for dipping

In a small bowl, add yogurt, protein, nut butter, extract, and coconut flour. Store well.

Top with chocolate chips and enjoy dipped with apple slices, ½ cup (85 g) sliced strawberries, or enjoy straight from a spoon.

Per serving, dip only
330 calories • 9 g fat • 12 g carbs • 4 g fiber • 41 g protein

Per serving, dip and apple
390 calories • 9 g fat • 25 g carbs • 7 g fiber • 41 g protein

Nourishment Breakdown

PROTEIN yogurt, powder	**FIBER** coconut flour, some in apple
FAT nut butter, chocolate	**CARB/STARCH** apple or berries

Chicken Crunch Wrap

This is an easy anytime meal with protein, veggies, and fat that guarantee blood sugar stability. I often use leftover grilled chicken but it also works if you use frozen high-protein veggie burgers, eggs, or even air-fried chicken nuggets. Top it with your favorite cheese and enjoy.

1 rectangular wrap

2 tablespoons (32 g) bruschetta, hummus, pizza sauce, salsa, or pesto

2 tablespoons (10 g) Parmesan or desired cheese

1 chicken breast, cooked, or any other leftover dinner protein

Desired veggies like lettuce, onion, or tomato

Heat a sprayed skillet over medium heat.

Add sauce, cheese, and chicken, and any other fixings to the middle of the wrap and any other fixings.

Fold the wrap in toward the middle in a clockwise motion until you have a crunch-wrap shape.

Place the messy folded side onto the hot skillet. Spray the top with avocado or olive oil and allow to cook until browned, about 2 to 3 minutes.

Flip with a spatula and brown the other side. Cut in half and enjoy.

Per serving per wrap with a chicken breast

350 calories • 10 g fat • 18 g carbs • 5 g fiber • 42 g protein

Nourishment Breakdown

PROTEIN chicken

FAT cheese, pesto

FIBER any veggie

CARB/STARCH wrap

Classic Chicken Salad

This is one of my favorite lunch meals, especially in the warmer months. I love to make-and-take this one in a cooler to the beach, lake, or poolside to cool off. This lunch has chicken, yogurt, nuts, and grapes for sweetness but it's all in balance so it won't spike your blood sugar at midday.

4 cooked chicken breasts,
 chopped or shredded

½ cup (115 g) nonfat plain
 Greek yogurt

2 teaspoons spicy or Dijon
 mustard, optional

1½ cups (225 g) red seedless
 grapes, halved

1 cup (120 g) celery,
 chopped small

½ cup (55 g) pecans, halved
 or chopped

1 teaspoon salt

½ teaspoon pepper

Add all ingredients to a large bowl and stir well.

Store in the fridge.

Per serving   237 calories • 75 g fat • 9 g carbs • 1 g fiber • 34.5 g protein

Nourishment Breakdown

PROTEIN chicken, yogurt	FAT pecans FIBER celery	CARB/STARCH grapes, but not a whole carb serving

Tuna Salad

This recipe is super light but high in protein and is delicious in a tuna melt. Choose a high fiber bread, or a wrap, a moderate-fat cheese, and veggies. I like sliced bell peppers. I also add a bit of sweet relish. Yes, there's a bit of sugar but it's not a full carb serving. Also, the protein and fiber more than offset the effect, so it won't affect your blood sugar levels. You can also add this to your lunch salad if you need a protein source too.

20 ounces (560 g) canned tuna

1 lemon, juiced

½ red onion, diced

4 celery stalks, diced

¼ teaspoon pepper

½ teaspoon salt

½ teaspoon garlic powder

2 tablespoons (30 g) sweet relish
    or 6 bread and butter pickle
    chips, diced

½ cup (115 g) nonfat
    Greek yogurt

Bread or wrap

Drain cans of tuna and add to a large bowl. Mash with a fork.

Add all other ingredients and stir well. Store in the fridge, good for a week.

Per serving   212 calories • 1 g fat • 7 g carbs • 1 g fiber • 35 g protein

Nourishment Breakdown

PROTEIN tuna, yogurt	FAT none	CARB/STARCH some in sweet relish, but not a whole carb serving
	FIBER celery, onion	

Dill Chicken Salad

A high-protein, on-the-go lunch. Depending on how hungry you are, the serving size is 1 to 2 cups. You can eat it on a sandwich with bread or another high-protein choice, on whole grain crackers, or put it in a salad to balance blood sugar. Add a half an apple with peanut butter on top for a fiber and fat source, and you'll feel full and satisfied all afternoon long.

4 cooked chicken breasts, chopped
½ cup (60 g) celery, diced small
⅓ cup (75 g) diced dill pickles or (82 g) relish
1 shallot, sliced thin
¼ cup (16 g) fresh dill, chopped
1 lemon, juiced
¼ teaspoon onion powder
¼ teaspoon garlic powder
½ teaspoon salt
¼ teaspoon pepper
1 tablespoon (11 g) Dijon or spicy brown mustard
¼ cup (60 ml) white wine vinegar
½ cup (115 g) nonfat Greek yogurt

Add all ingredients to a large bowl and stir well.

Store in the fridge.

Per serving   202 calories • 15 g fat • 6 g carbs • 15 g fiber • 36 g protein

Nourishment Breakdown

PROTEIN chicken, yogurt
FAT none (perfect with tortilla chips)

FIBER veggies, pickle
CARB/STARCH none

Savory Protein Toast

If you love savory foods, you'll enjoy this simple recipe. It has a caprese salad twist, but you can switch out the veggies and spices for a flavor change up. It's fun to experiment and see what you like best. I like a fried egg on top which adds a bit more fat and protein to keep my blood sugar in balance. Choose a high-protein, low-carb, or whole wheat bread.

1 piece of bread, toasted

½ cup (115 g) low-fat or full-fat cottage cheese

½ teaspoon everything but the bagel seasoning

½ tomato, sliced

½ avocado, sliced

1 tablespoon (15 ml) balsamic vinegar

Desired fresh basil to top

Start by plating your piece of toast.

Add cottage cheese, seasoning, tomato, avocado, balsamic, and top with fresh basil. Enjoy!

Per serving   300 calories • 10 g fat • 24 g carbs • 8 g fiber • 25 g protein

Nourishment Breakdown

PROTEIN cottage cheese
FAT avocado, cottage cheese if full fat

FIBER tomato, avocado
CARB/STARCH toast

Lunch

7

Simple Family Dinners

A BALANCED DINNER is vital for blood sugar management. It provides your body with the necessary nutrients to control hunger, prevent late-night snacking and function well at night while you're sleeping. During the day, it helps prevent spikes or crashes in blood sugar that can occur when you skip meals or occasionally choose the wrong foods. I've designed these recipes to be simple to make eating a healthy dinner doable each day. Remember, enjoying a meal with family and friends can also help to reduce stress, which helps keep blood sugar more optimized.

Rosemary Pot Roast

Pot roast and potatoes is one of my sentimental nostalgic comfort recipes. Anyone else? It makes me think of home and cozy childhood memories of family dinners. Food is more than just fuel, so I love to include comfort foods that are both healthy and nourishing. This recipe includes plenty of protein, vegetables, and enough fat, so it's not only delicious, it keeps your blood sugar stable long after you eat.

3 pounds (1359 g) chuck or round roast

14.5 ounces (324 g) diced tomatoes with oregano, basil, garlic

¼ cup (60 ml) coconut aminos or Worcestershire sauce

10 cloves garlic, fresh minced or 5 teaspoons of the jarred pre-minced

1 cup (235 ml) beef or chicken bone broth

1 teaspoon salt

1 teaspoon pepper

24 ounces (336 g) new or golden potatoes, chopped

4 large carrots, sliced

8 ounces (72 g) mushrooms, sliced

1 small white or yellow onion, chopped

4 sprigs fresh rosemary or 2 teaspoons dried

SLOW COOKER

Place meat in slow cooker. Add all other ingredients, fresh veggies, and rosemary. Cook on low 7 to 8 hours.

Once cooked, remove rosemary sprigs and discard.

Remove meat and slice if using round roast because it's lean, or shred if using chuck roast. It'll fall apart because of the higher fat.

INSTANT POT

Place all ingredients in an Instant Pot. Meat first, veggies, and rosemary on top.

Set to manual mode for 60 minutes on high pressure.

When time is up and cooker beeps, turn off and allow pressure to release naturally for 15 minutes.

After 15 minutes, use the quick pressure lever to release any remaining pressure. Carefully remove lid and transfer roast and veggies to a warm plate. Discard rosemary sprigs.

Per serving, 7 ounces (196 g) of round roast, and 1 cup (71 g) of veggies
472 calories • 11 g fat • 23 g carbs • 2 g fiber • 55 g protein

Per serving, 7 ounces (196 g) chuck roast, and 1 cup (71 g) of veggies
587 calories • 23 g fat • 23 g carbs • 2 g fiber • 56 g protein

Nourishment Breakdown

PROTEIN meat, bone broth
FAT meat

FIBER carrots, onion, mushroom
CARB/STARCH potatoes

Buffalo Chicken Chili

Comfort food doesn't have to be unhealthy. This chili is so flavorful, no one would suspect that it's a healthy and blood sugar friendly meal. It's loaded with protein from the chicken and the bone broth and brimming with minerals and nutrients. Fix it and forget it in the slow cooker or last minute in the Instant Pot, both work great!

3 chicken breasts, uncooked

1 red onion, chopped

4 celery stalks, thinly sliced

1 clove garlic, minced or
   1 teaspoon garlic powder

2 cups (475 ml) bone broth,
   chicken or beef

14 ounces (378 g) fire-roasted
   tomatoes

15 ounces (480 g) canned kidney
   or great northern beans,
   drained and rinsed

¼ cup (60 ml) buffalo hot sauce

2 tablespoons (14 g) ranch
   dressing powder or ranch
   seasoning

½ teaspoon pepper

8 ounces (225 g) chive and onion
   or plain cream cheese (dairy-
   free and reduced fat both
   work well)

SLOW COOKER

Place all ingredients in a slow cooker, in the order listed.

Cook on low 4 to 5 hours or high for 3 hours.

Remove chicken and chop or shred. Add back to slow cooker and stir well.

INSTANT POT

Place all ingredients in the Instant Pot in the order listed.
Cook on high for 15 minutes.

Turn off and allow pressure to naturally release for 10 minutes.

Use the quick-pressure lever to release any remaining pressure. Carefully remove lid. Remove chicken and chop or shred. Add back to Instant Pot and stir well.

TOPPING IDEAS

Green onions, fresh cilantro, avocado, blue cheese, and pickled onions.

Per serving without toppings

417 calories • 11 g fat • 19 g carbs • 6 g fiber • 47 g protein

Nourishment Breakdown

PROTEIN chicken and bone broth
FAT cream cheese and optional toppings

FIBER celery, onion, tomatoes
CARB/STARCH beans

Simple Family Dinners

Chicken Broccoli Bake

This dish is always a hit with the whole family. It's also easy to prep ahead of time for dinner. If you are nostalgic for casserole, this one is for you, and it's healthy, with protein, fat, and fiber. No sugar spikes here. It's also a great recipe to make to bring to a potluck dinner.

3 cups (213 g) broccoli florets, chopped

1 cup (225 g) low-fat or full-fat cottage cheese

3 cloves garlic, minced

1 tablespoon (15 ml) coconut aminos or Worcestershire sauce

1 yellow onion, diced

3 cups (420 g) chicken, cooked and shredded (rotisserie works great)

1 tablespoon (3 g) dried dill

1 tablespoon (7 g) onion powder

1 teaspoon salt

½ teaspoon pepper

2 cups (225 g) cheddar cheese, shredded and divided

1 cup (195 g) rice (I used organic white minute rice in microwave)

Preheat oven to 375°F (190°C, gas mark 5).

Cook or steam broccoli and set aside. I cooked mine in a covered glass bowl in the microwave for 5 minutes.

While that's cooking, place cottage cheese in a blender and blend on medium speed until smooth. I usually blend the whole container and pour it back into the container for storage in the fridge.

In a large skillet, add garlic, aminos, and onion. Cook until softened, about 5 minutes. Turn off the heat and set aside.

In a large bowl add cooked chicken, broccoli, onion mixture, blended cottage cheese, all seasonings, 1 cup (115 g) shredded cheddar, and rice. Stir well until all combined.

Pour mixture into a sprayed 9 x 13-inch (23 x 33-cm) glass baking dish. Sprinkle remaining cheese on top and bake for 20 minutes. Let sit for 5 minutes before serving.

Per serving   316 calories • 17 g fat • 10 g carbs • 2 g fiber • 35 g protein

Nourishment Breakdown

PROTEIN chicken, cottage cheese

FAT cheese

FIBER broccoli, onion

CARB/STARCH rice

Taco Casserole

This recipe is a crowd pleaser and family favorite. Black beans are such a great carb option for healthy blood sugar levels because they're packed with insoluble fiber, which helps with insulin sensitivity. I like to top each serving with shredded lettuce, fresh cilantro, pickled onions, and nonfat Greek yogurt as the sour cream. Yum!

1 pound (488 g) 93% lean ground turkey or beef

2 tablespoons (15 g) taco seasoning

15.5 ounces (325 g) canned black beans, drained and rinsed

16 ounces (500 g) salsa

1 cup (115 g) cheddar cheese, shredded

2 to 4 low-carb tortillas (I used 2 large)

Preheat oven to 350°F (180°C, or gas mark 4).

In a large skillet over medium heat, brown meat until crumbled and cooked through. Drain off any fat remaining.

Add taco seasoning and turn to low heat. Add beans and salsa, stir until combined.

Spray a 9 x 13-inch (23 x 33-cm) glass dish with avocado or olive oil and now it's time to layer.

Place half of the tortillas in the dish, then half of the meat mixture, and lastly ½ cup (58 g) cheese. Layer again with remaining ingredients.

Cover with foil, and bake for 20 to 25 minutes. Cut into 6 servings.

Per serving   393 calories • 13 g fat • 24 g carbs • 9 g fiber • 45 g protein

Nourishment Breakdown

PROTEIN meat	**FIBER** salsa, some in beans and tortillas	**CARB/STARCH** beans, tortillas
FAT meat, cheese		

Veggie Pesto Pasta

You'll love this pasta warm or cold. It's a great dish to bring to a summer BBQ. You can easily swap out veggies depending on your favorites and what's in season. I've tried this recipe with asparagus, zucchini, yellow squash, and peas, and all of them taste great. When picking out a pesto at the grocery store, try to find one with olive oil, since it has anti-inflammatory properties. The fat in the pesto and the cheese works in balance with the fiber found in the broccoli and chickpeas and protein in the chicken. You'll feel full and satisfied.

2 cups (142 g) broccoli, chopped small

10 ounces (190 g) grape tomatoes

1 red onion, chopped

2 chicken breasts (can use rotisserie)

16 ounces (160 g) chickpea, red lentil, or lupini pasta

1 teaspoon salt

½ teaspoon pepper

3 tablespoons (45 g) pesto

¼ cup (25 g) Parmesan, shredded or shaved

Fresh basil, optional

Preheat oven to 425°F (220°C or gas mark 7). Place veggies on a lined sheet pan and roast in the oven for 20 minutes or so. You can salt and pepper the veg, if desired.

While that's cooking, if chicken is raw, place chicken in a large stock pot and cover with water. Cook over high heat and bring to a boil. Once boiling, cover and turn to low heat and cook 15 minutes or until cooked through.

Remove chicken and shred or dice to desired size.

Add pasta to hot water and turn heat to high. Follow cook time on the pasta box and drain when cooked.

Add veggies, pasta, salt, pepper, and chicken to the empty stock pot. Add pesto and Parmesan and stir well. Garnish with fresh basil, if desired.

Per serving   317 calories • 6 g fat • 38 g carbs • 8 g fiber • 31 g protein

Nourishment Breakdown

PROTEIN chicken, some in pasta

FAT pesto, cheese

FIBER veggies, some in pasta

CARB/STARCH pasta

Italian Stuffed Peppers

Great for dinner and easy to prep ahead of time, this recipe features lean protein, moderate fat from the cheese topping and sausage, and fiber from the cauliflower rice and peppers. All of this works together for optimal plate balance. To make it fun, you can use red, yellow, and green peppers.

8 bell peppers, any color

1 pound (450 g) Italian chicken sausage

1 pound (450 g) lean ground chicken, turkey, or beef

½ cup (75 g) jarred mild banana pepper rings

1 cup (107 g) frozen riced cauliflower

2 teaspoons Italian seasoning

1 teaspoon garlic powder

½ teaspoon salt

¼ teaspoon pepper

6 ounces (195 g) tomato paste

½ cup (60 g) shredded mozzarella

½ cup (50 g) shredded or grated Parmesan

Preheat oven to 375°F (190°C, gas mark 5).

Cut the tops off the peppers. Remove and discard the stems, seeds, and membrane.

Place the peppers, cut-side up in a 9 x 13-inch (23 x 33-cm) baking dish and add a small amount of water to the bottom of the dish to cover the bottom of the pan.

Remove sausage casing by scoring with a knife longwise, peeling casing off, and discarding.

In a large skillet over medium heat, brown the sausage and ground meat until cooked through. Add banana pepper rings, cauliflower, spices, and tomato paste. Cook 10 minutes or so until all incorporated and cauliflower is cooked through.

Stuff the peppers by adding about ½ cup of the meat mixture to each. Evenly distribute the cheese over the top of the stuffed peppers.

Cook covered for 30 minutes. (I sprayed the foil with avocado oil spray to prevent the cheese from sticking.) Remove foil, cook 10 more minutes and enjoy!

Per serving of 1 pepper with 99% lean ground turkey

237 calories • 7 g fat • 12 g carbs • 5 g fiber • 29 g protein

Nourishment Breakdown

PROTEIN chicken sausage, ground meat
FAT cheese, some in sausage

FIBER peppers, cauliflower, tomato paste
CARB/STARCH none

Sausage Lentil Stew

This is a nourishing comfort meal that's easy to prepare in your slow cooker. Just put in the ingredients in the morning and you'll have a balanced blood sugar dinner when you get home. Lentils are a high-quality carb/starch source loaded with fiber, and even contain some plant-based protein. They also have essential nutrients like folate, iron, calcium, magnesium, potassium, and zinc. I like using ground turkey breakfast sausage in this one. Whatever you choose, cut it into coins first before adding to the slow cooker. Delish!

1 pound (450 g) Italian chicken sausage, ground, or fresh links with casings removed

2 cups (384 g) green or brown lentils

1 yellow onion, chopped

1 cup (100 g) celery, diced

1 cup (130 g) carrots, chopped

14.5 ounces (324 g) canned diced tomatoes

3 cloves garlic, minced

4 cups (950 ml) chicken or beef bone broth

1 bay leaf

1 teaspoon cumin

½ teaspoon pepper

½ teaspoon salt

2 tablespoons (30 ml) red wine vinegar

OPTIONAL TOPPINGS
Fresh basil, Parmesan cheese

In a large skillet over medium heat, brown the sausage until crumbled and cooked through. Set aside.

In a slow cooker, add cooked sausage, and all remaining ingredients except the vinegar.

Cook on low 6 to 8 hours or high 3 to 4. Low is optimal, if you have the time.

Once cooked, remove the bay leaf and add the red wine vinegar. Allow to cook 15 more minutes and enjoy!

Per serving with 2 tablespoons (10 g) Parmesan

357 calories • 8 g fat • 44 g carbs • 13 g fiber • 40 g protein

Nourishment Breakdown

PROTEIN sausage, lentils	**FIBER** lentils, veggies
FAT sausage, cheese	**CARB/STARCH** lentils

Chicken Spinach Artichoke Bake

This simple recipe is a perfect high-protein and high-fiber option to bring as an appetizer or dip for parties and get-togethers. Or you can cook it as-is and have it for a weeknight dinner. Either way, you'll be eating for optimal blood sugar balance.

3 cups (420 g) cooked and shredded chicken breasts (rotisserie works great)

1 cup (186 g) rice, cooked and cooled

12-ounce (450-g) jarred or canned artichoke (in water, not oil), drained and chopped

10 ounces (38 g) frozen spinach (can thaw first or use frozen)

1 cup (225 g) low-fat cottage cheese

½ cup (115 g) nonfat or 2% Greek yogurt

1 cup (115 g) shredded mozzarella

½ teaspoon each salt and pepper

1 teaspoon garlic powder

½ teaspoon dried basil

Preheat oven to 400°F (200°C, or gas mark 6).

Combine all ingredients in a large bowl and stir well.

Pour into a 9 x 13-inch (23 x 33-cm) glass dish and bake for 25 to 30 minutes. Switch to broil high for 2 to 3 minutes to brown the top. Watch it so it doesn't burn.

Let it stand for 5 to 10 minutes or so before eating. The steam from the spinach has to soak in.

Per serving   315 calories • 9 g fat • 15 g carbs • 2 g fiber • 42 g protein

Nourishment Breakdown

PROTEIN cottage cheese, yogurt, chicken
FAT mozzarella

FIBER spinach, artichokes
CARB/STARCH rice but still not a whole serving

Tuna Cakes

Delicious with vegetables and a baked potato, you can also put these cakes in a wrap and add cheese as a topping for a tuna melt. Whether you make this for dinner or on-the-go lunch, you'll be eating a high-quality protein that will keep your energy up and sugar spikes away.

10 ounces (280 g) canned
  tuna, drained
¼ cup (60 g) nonfat
  Greek yogurt
2 tablespoons (22 g)
  Dijon mustard
2 teaspoons garlic, minced
2 eggs, lightly beaten
½ teaspoon salt
¼ teaspoon pepper
½ cup (8 oz) fresh cilantro,
  chopped
1 tablespoon (14 g) butter
  for frying

First, make sure you've drained the tuna really well. Then, in a medium-sized bowl use a fork to mix tuna and all other ingredients, except butter. Stir well.

In a large skillet over medium heat, add butter to coat the pan.

With a ⅓ cup (38 g) sized measuring cup, dollop the batter into cakes in the frying pan. Cover and cook about 5 minutes or until golden brown and flip to cook other side.

Serve immediately. I love to squeeze fresh lemon juice over before eating and these are great for a protein meal prep for the week too. Store in the fridge.

Per cake 370 calories • 8 g fat • 1 g carbs • 30 g protein

Nourishment Breakdown

PROTEIN tuna, yogurt, egg	**FIBER** cilantro	
FAT yolk, butter	**CARB/STARCH** none	

High-Protein Alfredo

My teenagers and their friends all love this recipe. You'd never know it's not the real deal Alfredo sauce and is mostly made from cottage cheese. It takes 15 minutes from start to finish so it's a great quick dinner option for any night. I try to have all the ingredients always on hand so I can whip some up anytime they request it. It's high-protein and high-fiber, with some fat for optimal plate balance.

16 ounces (456 g) red lentil or chickpea pasta (for lower carb use 2 cans/boxes of hearts of palm pasta)

1 cup (235 ml) unsweetened almond milk (cashew or coconut works too)

2 cups (450 g) low-fat cottage cheese

1 teaspoon cornstarch

½ teaspoon each salt and pepper

½ teaspoon Italian seasoning

½ teaspoon garlic powder

½ cup (50 g) grated Parmesan cheese

Fresh parsley to top, optional

First, cook pasta as the box directions suggest.

Meanwhile, put all other remaining ingredients (except pasta and parsley) in the blender and blend until smooth.

Pour sauce into a sprayed saucepan or skillet over medium or low heat. Cook until heated through (about 5 minutes) and stir often.

Add cooked and drained pasta to sauce and toss to soak up the sauce. Garnish with parsley and serve immediately.

Great with veggies and/or a salad. Plenty of protein as-is but of course add shrimp, chicken, or even veggies, if desired.

Per serving with chickpea pasta
406 calories • 9 g fat • 53 g carbs • 8 g fiber • 35 g protein

Per serving with hearts of palm pasta
126 calories • 4 g fat • 19 g carbs • 3 g fiber • 17 g protein
(Super low calorie but good for an appetizer, or have larger portions depending on hunger)

Nourishment Breakdown

PROTEIN cottage cheese, pasta

FAT parmesan cheese

FIBER pasta

CARB/STARCH pasta

Balanced Meal Chili

This great tasting, crowd pleasing recipe has won two chili cook-offs over the years and is blood sugar friendly too. Best of all, it's super simple to make. Although you can't taste the pumpkin, it makes this chili thick and decadent, and adds nutrients like vitamin A. This is a comfort food recipe you'll return to again and again.

1 red or white onion, chopped

2 cloves garlic, minced

2 pounds (900 g) ground beef, chicken, turkey, or a combo

1 teaspoon pepper

1 tablespoon (3 g) oregano

2 tablespoons (14 g) chili powder

2 tablespoons (14 g) cumin

¼ cup (60 ml) coconut aminos

15 ounces (225 g) canned pumpkin

15 ounces (460 g) canned tomato sauce

15 ounces (338 g) canned diced tomatoes

15.5 ounces (434 g) canned great northern beans (rinsed and drained)

In a large Dutch oven over medium heat, add diced onions and garlic, cook for a few minutes to soften, and add meat.

Cook until brown and crumbled, add spices, then add all other remaining ingredients. Bring to a boil, then cover and cook on low heat for 20 minutes.

SLOW COOKER

Brown onion, garlic, and meat in a skillet over medium heat.

Once browned and crumbled, add meat mixture and remaining ingredients to the slow cooker and cook on low for 3 to 6 hours.

Per serving with 93% lean organic beef

370 calories • 10 g fat • 22 g carbs • 8 g fiber • 37 g protein

Nourishment Breakdown

PROTEIN meat	**FIBER** onion, pumpkin,	**CARB/STARCH** beans,
FAT meat	beans, tomatoes	pumpkin

Caprese Sheet Pan

This sheet pan recipe is so simple and full of flavor. You can add this quick protein and healthy fat option to a salad, veggie, or potato for an optimumly balanced meal. Marinating the chicken overnight gives it more flavor. In a pinch, at least 30 minutes will work too.

MARINADE

4 chicken breasts

¼ cup (60 ml) balsamic vinegar

1 tablespoon (11 g) honey
   Dijon mustard

1 teaspoon garlic powder or
   1 clove garlic, minced

2 teaspoons Italian seasoning

½ teaspoon salt

¼ teaspoon pepper

TOPPINGS

2 large tomatoes, sliced

8 ounces (115 g) fresh
   mozzarella, divided

Fresh basil

First marinate the chicken. Place chicken in a shallow dish or large plastic bag. Add all marinade ingredients to chicken and make sure all pieces are covered well.

Seal dish or bag and place in the refrigerator for at least 30 minutes or overnight.

When ready to cook, preheat oven to 400°F (200°C, or gas mark 6) and place marinaded chicken on a lined or sprayed sheet pan. Place one tomato slice and 2 ounces (29 g) of fresh mozzarella to the top of the chicken.

Bake at for 25 to 30 minutes or until the internal temperature of the chicken is 165°F (74°C), and done. Serve with fresh basil on top.

Per chicken breast

323 calories • 7 g fat • 25 g carbs • 0 g fiber • 53 g protein

Nourishment Breakdown

PROTEIN chicken	**FIBER** none
FAT mozzarella	**CARB/STARCH** none

Balanced Zuppa Toscana

This meal is super comforting and nourishing thanks to the protein in the chicken and minerals in the bone broth. It's gluten-free, dairy-free, and has a great balance of nutrients for a happy tummy and stable blood sugar.

2 pounds (908 g) chicken breasts, cutlets, or tenders

24 ounces (335 g) gold potatoes, cut into bite-size pieces (can use less if wanting lower carb)

3 cloves garlic, minced

1 onion, diced

½ teaspoon crushed red pepper (can use less if sensitive to spice)

2 teaspoons Italian seasoning

½ teaspoon salt

¼ teaspoon pepper

4 cups (950 ml) bone broth, chicken or beef

13-ounce (380-ml) can unsweetened coconut milk

5 pieces uncured bacon, cooked and crumbled

3 cups (200 g) kale, thick stems removed and chopped, or buy an already prepped bag

Place chicken in a slow cooker, then add potatoes, garlic, onion, seasonings, and broth.

Cook on low heat 4 to 7 hours or high heat 3 hours.

Remove chicken and shred or dice and put back in the slow cooker.

Add coconut milk, bacon, and kale. Turn to high and cook for 15 minutes or until kale is cooked and tender.

Per serving   437 calories • 17 g fat • 21 g carbs • 3 g fiber • 42 g protein

Nourishment Breakdown

PROTEIN chicken, bone broth

FAT coconut milk, bacon

FIBER kale, onion

CARB/STARCH potatoes

Quick Loaded Chicken Nachos

This is a perfect last-minute dinner that's ready in minutes if you start with a rotisserie chicken. You can get creative with toppings or keep it simple. The protein in the chicken will offset the carbs in the chips to keep blood sugar levels in check. You can also use bell peppers, which add fiber to this dish. I usually double this recipe if my whole family is eating.

2 cups (280 g) rotisserie chicken breasts (both breasts, skin removed)

½ cup (125 g) salsa

½ teaspoon taco seasoning

3 servings (84 g) tortilla chips

2 bell peppers, any color, cut into chip size

1 cup (115 g) Mexican blend shredded cheese

OPTIONAL TOPPINGS (AFTER COOKED)

Sour cream or Greek yogurt, shredded lettuce, fresh cilantro, black olives, jalapeños, lime juice

Preheat oven to 400°F (200°C, or gas mark 6).

Shred or dice chicken and place in a bowl. Add salsa and taco seasoning, stir well and set aside.

On a lined or sprayed sheet pan, place bell pepper pieces and chips to line the pan. Add chicken and shredded cheese.

Cook for 5 to 10 minutes or until cheese is melted. Top with desired toppings and enjoy!

Per serving without toppings

360 calories • 15 g fat • 21 g carbs • 3 g fiber • 30 g protein

Nourishment Breakdown

PROTEIN chicken

FAT cheese, chips

FIBER bell pepper

CARB/STARCH chips

Balanced Chicken Tetrazzini

Who doesn't love a one-dish casserole that's a blood sugar balanced meal? This is easy to put together, especially if you start with a rotisserie chicken, which is your protein source. The fat is in the cheese sauce, and you'll find fiber in the chickpeas and red lentils. Remember serving sizes are just suggestions, so always go by your individual hunger and fullness cues.

2 chicken breasts
(can use rotisserie)

8 ounces (72 g) sliced
mushrooms

2 tablespoons (30 g)
coconut aminos

16 ounces (160 g) chickpea,
red lentil, or lupini pasta

1 cup (235 ml) unsweetened
almond milk (cashew or
coconut works too)

2 cups (450 g) low-fat
cottage cheese

1 teaspoon cornstarch

½ teaspoon pepper

1 teaspoon salt

½ teaspoon parsley

½ teaspoon garlic powder

½ cup (50 g) grated
Parmesan cheese

1 cup (115 g) shredded
mozzarella or Italian
blend cheese

Preheat oven to 350°F (180°C, or gas mark 4). If chicken is raw, place chicken in a large stock pot and cover with water. Cook over high heat and bring to a boil, cover, and turn to low heat and cook 15 minutes or until cooked through.

While chicken is cooking, put a large skillet over medium heat. Add mushrooms and aminos. Stir occasionally and cook 10 to 15 minutes. Turn off heat. Set aside.

Once chicken is cooked, remove chicken and shred or diced to desired size. Set aside.

Add pasta to hot water and turn heat to high. Follow cooking instructions on the pasta box and drain when cooked.

While pasta is cooking, make the cheese sauce by adding milk, cottage cheese, cornstarch, seasonings, and Parmesan to the blender and blend until smooth.

In the large stock pot, add the pasta, chicken mixture, and cheese sauce. Stir to combine and pour into a sprayed 9 x 13-inch (23 x 33-cm) glass baking dish and add the 1 cup (115 g) mozzarella cheese to the top.

Bake uncovered for 20 to 25 minutes.

Per serving   439 calories • 10 g fat • 44 g carbs • 7 g fiber • 48 g protein

Nourishment Breakdown

PROTEIN some in pasta, chicken, sauce

FAT cheese

FIBER mushrooms, some in pasta

CARB/STARCH pasta

Mediterranean Beef Stew

I love this comforting meal, and it only takes about 10 minutes to put together in the slow cooker in the morning. You can fix it and forget it and come home to a wonderful aroma. If you're not feeling well, this is a good choice thanks to all the nutrients and minerals in the meat, veggies, and bone broth. For tender meat, I recommend cooking on low for 6 to 8 hours.

2 pounds (900 g) lean stew meat

5 cloves garlic, minced

1 yellow onion, diced

1 cup (100 g) celery, diced

1 cup (130 g) carrots, diced

14.5 ounces (324 g) canned diced tomatoes

15 ounces (450 g) canned chickpeas/garbanzo beans, drained

1 bay leaf

1 teaspoon oregano

1 teaspoon salt

½ teaspoon pepper

2 cups (475 ml) bone broth, chicken or beef

½ cup (30 g) fresh parsley, whole stems

2 cups (134 g) kale, destemmed and chopped

TOPPINGS

Feta, crumbled

Place cubed stew meat at the bottom of the slow cooker.

Add remaining ingredients (except kale).

Set to low and cover. Cook for 6 to 8 hours.

About 30 minutes before eating, remove the parsley and discard. Add the kale and cover to cook 30 more minutes or until kale is tender.

Per serving without feta
284 calories • 105 g fat • 19 g carbs • 5 g fiber • 26 g protein

Per serving with ¼ cup (38 g) feta
384 calories • 185 g fat • 20 g carbs • 5 g fiber • 32 g protein

Nourishment Breakdown

PROTEIN beef
FAT beef, cheese
FIBER veggies
CARB/STARCH chickpeas/garbanzo beans

Ranch Chicken

Who doesn't love a slow cooker easy dinner recipe? This crowd pleaser has only four ingredients so you can't go wrong. To make it part of a blood sugar balanced dish, add the chicken to a salad or wrap. Make it a meal by including a vegetable, and a carb like a baked potato. My kids love ranch chicken on buns, as sliders, or quesadillas. I top mine with pickled onions. Your taste buds will never get bored!

3 pounds (1362 g) chicken breasts or turkey tenderloins

2 tablespoons (15 g) ranch powder packet, or
1 tablespoon (7 g) of ranch seasoning works too

8 ounces (225 g) light or regular cream cheese

1 cup (235 ml) bone broth

Place all ingredients in a slow cooker in the order listed and cook on high 3 to 4 hours or low for 6 to 8 hours.

Once cooked, shred with a fork or use a hand mixer to shred chicken. Add back to slow cooker and stir into sauce.

Per serving with light cream cheese

317 calories • 6 g fat • 1 g carbs • 46 g protein

Nourishment Breakdown

PROTEIN chicken/turkey, broth	**FIBER** none
FAT cream cheese	**CARB/STARCH** none

Pad Thai

This recipe is delicious and gives you an optimal plate balance. It's chock full of vegetables. In fact, you'll get three of your daily servings in one meal and plenty of fiber too. Tofu can be your protein source, but in a pinch you can use shrimp or chicken.

4 ounces (114 g) organic extra-firm tofu, drained and diced (or 1 pound [454 g] chicken breast, diced in 1-inch [2.5-cm] pieces, or shrimp, or a combo)

3 cloves garlic, minced

2 teaspoons minced ginger

1 teaspoon salt

½ yellow onion, diced

1 red bell pepper, sliced thin

2 carrots, chopped

3 eggs

24 ounces (450 g) hearts of palm noodles, konjac noodles, or 1 cooked spaghetti squash

SAUCE

2 tablespoons (30 g) low-sugar ketchup

2 tablespoons (30 ml) coconut aminos

¼ cup (60 ml) chicken bone broth or vegetable broth if vegan

2 tablespoons (30 ml) rice vinegar

2 tablespoons (30 g) fish sauce

1 tablespoon (15 ml) lime juice (about 1 lime)

1 tablespoon (16 g) natural peanut butter

1 tablespoon (15 g) sriracha, optional

1 teaspoon molasses or monk fruit/stevia, optional

OPTIONAL TOPPINGS

½ cup (8 g) cilantro, torn or chopped

2 green onions, chopped

2 tablespoons (18 g) salted peanuts

1 teaspoon red pepper flakes

In a large skillet or wok over medium high heat, add diced tofu (or preferred protein) and cook until cooked through. Shrimp and tofu take 3 to 4 minutes each side and chicken takes a bit longer. You can add salt and pepper, if desired. I sprayed my pan with avocado oil spray.

FOR THE SAUCE

While that's cooking, make the sauce in a medium bowl by combining all sauce ingredients and whisk until combined. Cook the pasta according to package directions and drain, or shred squash.

Set cooked protein aside on a plate. Add garlic, ginger, salt, onion, bell pepper, and carrot to the heated skillet and cook on medium heat until tender. You can salt and pepper the veggies too, if desired.

Push the veggies aside in the skillet and break the 3 eggs on the other half of the pan to scramble.

Add noodles or squash to the skillet with veggies and eggs. Add protein and sauce. Stir to combine. Serve with desired toppings.

Per serving with tofu only

204 calories • 8 g fat • 16 g carbs • 4 g fiber • 13 g protein

Per serving with tofu and 1 pound (454 g) chicken

352 calories • 11 g fat • 16 g carbs • 4 g fiber • 42 g protein

Per serving with 1 pound (454 g) chicken (shrimp is similar to chicken)

271 calories • 7 g fat • 16 g carbs • 4 g fiber • 29 g protein

Nourishment Breakdown

PROTEIN tofu, eggs, chicken/shrimp FIBER pasta, veggies
FAT eggs, peanut, tofu CARB/STARCH none

Sheet Pan Shawarma

This recipe is simple yet so full of flavor. You can prep this ahead of time and create a self-serve bowl bar at a get-together with all the topping options. I love to eat it over a bed of salad greens with tzatziki dip as a dressing. If you're not a thigh fan, you can swap for breasts, but you'll need the feta, olives, or maybe some hummus to add healthy fats to your balanced meal.

10 boneless skinless
    chicken thighs

1 cup (230 g) nonfat
    Greek yogurt

2 lemons, juiced

5 cloves garlic, minced

1 teaspoon salt

½ teaspoon pepper

2 teaspoons cumin

2 teaspoons paprika

1 teaspoon turmeric

½ teaspoon cinnamon

Desired red pepper
    flakes, optional

2 red bell peppers, sliced

1 red onion, sliced

Fresh parsley for garnish

Cut chicken thighs into 1-inch (2.5-cm) pieces and place in a large dish or gallon size bag.

To make the marinade, add yogurt, lemon, garlic, and spices. Massage into chicken and marinate 30 minutes or 24 hours in the fridge.

Preheat oven to 425°F (220°C or gas mark 7). Add chicken to a sprayed or lined sheet pan and cook for 10 minutes.

While that's cooking, chop up veggies. Add veggies to the top of the chicken and cook 20–25 more minutes. Top with parsley. Serve over cauliflower rice, a salad, or in a low-carb pita.

FOR SERVING, OPTIONAL
Tzatziki sauce, hummus, tomatoes chopped, feta cheese crumbled, olives, cucumber slices, low-carb pita/tortilla, salad, cauliflower rice

---

Per serving   298 calories • 9 g fat • 4 g carbs • 1 g fiber • 44 g protein

Nourishment Breakdown

PROTEIN chicken thighs	**FAT** chicken thighs, feta (if adding)	**CARB/STARCH** none or pita/tortilla (if adding)
	FIBER onion, bell pepper	

Balanced Basic Taco Night

If you eat out or in, the main thing to be mindful of when eating tacos is to make it a balanced meal, with protein, fats, and fiber. I usually choose lean meats because guacamole, chips, cheese, and sour cream are all high in fat. If you prefer full-fat red meat, just make it your only fat source. I love to double this recipe so the kids can have nachos with the leftover meat the next day.

2 pounds (900 g) ground chicken, turkey, or lean beef

1 tablespoon (7 g) taco seasoning

15 ounces (460 g) canned tomato sauce

1 cup (107 g) frozen riced cauliflower

OPTIONAL ADD INS
Lettuce for a taco salad or taco/nacho topping, diced tomatoes, low-carb tortillas or corn tortillas, tortilla chips, sour cream or nonfat Greek yogurt, cheese, guac or sliced avocado, salsa

Brown meat in a large skillet until cooked through.

Add taco seasoning, tomato sauce, and cauliflower. Cook 5 to 10 minutes, stirring occasionally and cover the pan, if desired, to speed up the cauliflower cooking time. You want the cauliflower cooked through so it's hidden. Serve with your desired serving of carb/starch (tortilla or chips) or skip it! I love to do a big salad with a few crumbled chips as a topping for a crunch.

Per serving   192 calories • 2 g fat • 6 g carbs • 15 g fiber • 35 g protein

Nourishment Breakdown
PROTEIN meat, Greek yogurt (if using)
FAT meat, cheese, guac, chips
FIBER cauliflower, lettuce, tomatoes
CARB/STARCH chips, tortillas

Chicken Philly Sheet Pan

This is a great choice if you need to get dinner ready in 30 minutes or less. There's no starch so enjoy the dish on a toasted sub, low-carb tortilla, crunch wrap, or skip your starch and have it over a salad or in a riced cauliflower bowl.

2 pounds (908 g) chicken tenderloins, cut into 1-inch (2.5-cm) pieces (about 5 pieces per tender)

8 ounces (72 g) mushrooms, sliced

2 bell peppers (any color), sliced thin

½ red onion, sliced thin

1 teaspoon garlic powder or 2 cloves minced

½ teaspoon smoked paprika

1 teaspoon Italian seasoning

1 teaspoon salt

¼ teaspoon pepper

8 ounces (232 g) provolone slices

Preheat oven to 400°F (200°C, or gas mark 6).

Place cut chicken pieces on half of a lined or sprayed sheet pan and place sliced veggies on the other half.

Spray all with oil. Add all seasonings evenly over chicken and veggies mixture.

Bake for 20 minutes or until chicken is cooked through. Remove pan from oven and add cheese slices to the top of veggies and chicken.

Place back in oven and turn to broil high for 2 to 4 minutes. Watch it because it'll burn quickly. Broil until desired melty-ness is achieved.

Per serving   350 calories • 10 g fat • 4 g carbs • 1 g fiber • 38 g protein

Nourishment Breakdown

PROTEIN chicken   **FIBER** veggies

FAT cheese, oil (a little)   **CARB/STARCH** none or add bread

8

Power Bowls

Y OU CAN MAKE all of these recipes ahead of time for a quick lunch or dinner during the week. A little meal prep can save time in the long run and you'll be able to eat right away when hunger strikes. This is much better than allowing your growling stomach to call the shots and grabbing less nutritious snacks or take out. Knowing you have meals ready to go can also reduce stress and decision fatigue related to mealtimes. When you prep meals ahead of time, it also helps with portion control which is important for blood sugar balance.

Pizza Power Bowls

Perfect to prep ahead of time for a family dinner. It's super light so you can eat a bigger portion if you like. To make it more filling, you can add a package of cauliflower rice and regular rice for a carb source. Kids also like rice as part of dinner. Either way, you have lots of healthy options to ensure blood sugar stability for the evening and boost the next day's reserves as well.

8 ounces (72 g) sliced
  mushrooms
½ red onion, sliced thin
1 green bell pepper, sliced
1 teaspoon salt, divided
¾ teaspoon pepper, divided
1 teaspoon garlic powder,
  divided
1 teaspoon Italian
  seasoning, divided
20 ounces (260 g) frozen
  riced cauliflower
2 pounds (900 g) lean
  ground turkey
8 large or 32 small uncured beef
  and pork pepperoni
13 ounces (406 g) pizza sauce
½ cup (58 g) mozzarella,
  shredded
¼ cup (25 g) Parmesan, grated
  or (38 g) feta, crumbled

OPTIONAL TOPPINGS
Banana pepper rings
Black olives, sliced
Red pepper flakes

In a large skillet over medium heat, add mushrooms, onion, and bell pepper. Season with ½ teaspoon each salt, pepper, garlic powder, and Italian seasoning.

Cook about 5 minutes, until softened.

Add frozen riced cauliflower, stir, and cover.

In another large skillet, brown the ground turkey until cooked through. Season with remaining spices.

Combine vegetable and meat mixtures, then divide equally among 6 covered bowls. Add pepperoni and pour pizza sauce and cheese over meat mixture and cover to melt the cheese.

Per serving 310 calories • 10 g fat • 9 g carbs • 3.5 g fiber • 45 g protein

Nourishment Breakdown

PROTEIN turkey, pepperoni	**FIBER** veggies
FAT cheese, pepperoni	**CARB/STARCH** none or rice if using

Buffalo Power Bowls

Easy to prep ahead of time, this is a great dish that enables you to build your own optimum balanced bowl for dinner. The crunch of the celery, the tangy ranch dressing, and the spicy chicken is a yummy combo. Each serving has about 2 cups (142 g) of veggies, which improves gut health thanks to the fiber and prebiotics each contains. Want more healthy fats? Add ¼ fresh avocado to the top.

MEAT

4 boneless chicken breasts

1 cup (235 ml) buffalo hot sauce. If sensitive to heat, do ½ cup (120 ml) of sauce and ½ cup (120 ml) bone broth

2 tablespoons (30 ml) coconut aminos or Worcestershire sauce

1 clove garlic, minced

BOWL BASE AND TOPPINGS

(Some optional, add what you like)

Two 10-ounce (284-g) bags slaw

4 ounces (80 g) blue cheese crumbles

1 celery stalk, diced

1 bunch green onions, diced

½ red onion, diced

If wanting a starch, add diced potatoes or rice

Ranch dressing (*see recipe*) or buy store bought

Place chicken breasts in a slow cooker and cover with hot sauce/broth, then add garlic and aminos/Worchestershire sauce.

Cook on low 4 to 6 hours and shred chicken when cooked through. Add back to slow cooker.

To each of 5 covered bowls, add 1½ cups (340 g) of slaw, 1 cup (140 g) cooked chicken, the celery, ½ green onion (white and light green part), 2 tablespoons (16 g) cheese, and cover with ¼ cup (60 ml) ranch dressing.

Per bowl with all the fixings and dressing

461 calories • 10 g fat • 10 g carbs • 3 g fiber • 54 g protein

Nourishment Breakdown

PROTEIN chicken	**FIBER** veggies
FAT cheese	**CARB/STARCH** none

Ranch Dressing

1 cup (225 g) cottage cheese

2 tablespoons (15 g) ranch dressing powder or ½ teaspoon each dill, parsley, onion powder, garlic powder, salt, dash of pepper

½ cup (120 ml) buttermilk

½ lemon, juiced

Blend all ingredients in a blender.

Per serving

30 calories • 1 g fat

2 g carbs • 5 g protein

Fish Taco Power Bowls

For this recipe I used frozen, wild-caught mahi-mahi thawed out overnight in the refrigerator, as per the package instructions. But any white fish works great! This recipe is so full of flavor, fiber, and protein, you'll feel full and satisfied. If you'd like to add a carb/starch source, choose a tortilla or a serving of tortilla chips. The turmeric is a bonus because it reduces inflammation in the body. It also has a super mild taste so it's a great addition to any savory dish.

FISH

Five 5-ounce (140-g)
    white fish fillets

2 teaspoons taco seasoning

2 teaspoons seafood seasoning

1 clove garlic, minced

20 ounces (260 g) frozen
    cauliflower rice or (488 g)
    regular brown rice

½ teaspoon turmeric

Dash of cumin

½ teaspoon salt

¼ teaspoon pepper

6-ounce (195-g) can
    tomato paste

Quick slaw (Mexican flavor)
    on page 159

OPTIONAL TOPPINGS

Cotija cheese, crumbled

Fresh cilantro

Lime juice

Preheat oven to 400°F (200°C, or gas mark 6).

Place the fish on a lined sheet pan. Season evenly with taco and seafood seasoning.

Bake for 20 to 30 minutes or until internal temperature is 145°F (63°C) and done.

While the fish is cooking, use a large skillet over medium heat and add minced garlic and frozen cauliflower rice. Stir and cover for 5 minutes or so.

Season the rice with all the spices and seasonings and stir well. Cook covered until it's cooked through, about 10 to 15 minutes. Set aside.

In a large bowl, stir all quick slaw ingredients together until well combined.

To assemble the 5 power bowls, add ½ cup (54 g) cauliflower or (93 g) brown rice mixture, 1½ cups (340 g) slaw, 5 ounces (140 g) of fish, and 1 ounce (28 g) Cotija cheese crumbled into each container.

Per bowl with 1 ounce of cheese

347 calories • 9 g fat • 15 g carbs • 6 g fiber • 45 g protein

Nourishment Breakdown

PROTEIN fish	FIBER slaw, cauli-	CARB/STARCH none
FAT cheese	flower, tomato paste	

The Blood Sugar Balance Cookbook

Mediterranean Power Bowls

I always like having prepped, balanced, feel-good meals ready in the fridge. You can prep this dish in the slow cooker, blend in the cucumber and tomato salad, and build your own balanced bowl for dinner. My kids like to add rice to theirs. You won't need to add salt thanks to all the flavors in this recipe.

MEAT MIXTURE

4 chicken breasts

5 ounces (450 g) canned chickpeas, drained

6 ounces (174 g) pitted kalamata olives, drained

16 ounces (300 g) roasted red bell pepper strips, drained

¼ cup (34 g) capers

1 tablespoon Italian seasoning

2 teaspoons garlic powder or 2 cloves, minced

½ teaspoon pepper

CUCUMBER TOMATO SALAD

10 ounces (190 g) grape tomatoes, sliced in half

1 pound (240 g) mini or regular cucumbers, sliced

½ red onion, sliced thin

2 lemons, juiced

¼ cup (60 ml) red wine vinegar

½ cup (20 g) fresh basil, minced

½ cup (75 g) feta, crumbled

½ teaspoon salt

¼ teaspoon pepper

½ teaspoon Italian seasoning

OPTIONAL TOPPING

2 tablespoons (30 g) tzatziki dip or sauce, store bought

FOR MEAT MIXTURE

Place chicken at the bottom of the slow cooker with all other meat ingredients.

Cook on low 4 hours or high for 2 hours. Once chicken is cooked through, shred it and add back to slow cooker.

FOR CUCUMBER TOMATO SALAD

To make the salad, add all salad ingredients to a bowl and stir.

Assemble each bowl by adding ½ cup of the salad and 1½ cups (336 g) of the meat mixture. Top with tzatziki sauce, if desired.

Per bowl   419 calories • 15 g fat • 24 g carbs • 6 g fiber • 46 g protein

Nourishment Breakdown

PROTEIN chicken, some in chickpeas

FAT cheese, olives

FIBER peppers, cucumbers, tomatoes, some in chickpeas

CARB/STARCH chickpeas

Sriracha Salmon Power Bowls

If you can find wild-caught salmon, that's the best option because it contains potent omega 3 fats that are good for your brain and blood sugar balance. It's also a complete protein source. We love to eat this one cold like sushi but it's also a great dinner recipe for the family. You can also cook the salmon in the air fryer at 400°F (200°C) for about 5 minutes.

MARINADE

2 pounds (896 g) wild-caught salmon fillets (I used frozen and thawed)

¼ cup (60 ml) coconut aminos

¼ cup (60 ml) sriracha

3 cloves garlic, minced

¼ cup (60 ml) water

SLAW

24 ounces (620 g) shelled edamame, frozen

12 ounces (340 g) coleslaw

3 green onions, chopped (white and light green part)

¼ cup (60 ml) rice vinegar

½ cup (115 g) nonfat Greek yogurt

½ teaspoon salt

¼ teaspoon pepper

½ teaspoon ginger

OPTIONAL BOWL ADD-INS

1 cucumber, sliced

Everything but the bagel seasoning

Black sesame seeds

Green onion

More sriracha

TO MAKE MARINADE

First, cut salmon into 1-inch (2.5-cm) pieces and remove skin, if desired. Place in a large bowl and add marinade ingredients. Stir and cover.

Place in the fridge to marinate while you make the slaw.

TO MAKE SLAW

Cook frozen edamame according to package directions. In a large bowl, add edamame and all other slaw ingredients and stir well.

TO ASSEMBLE

In a large sprayed skillet over medium heat, add salmon and marinade. I did mine in two batches. Cook 3 to 4 minutes on each side until 145°F (63°C) internal temperature is reached.

Assemble the bowls by adding 1 cup (227 g) of the slaw and 5 ounces (140 g) of the salmon (about 10 pieces). Add cucumber and toppings, if desired. If this is dinner and not an adult meal prep, I add rice for the kids if you'd like them to have more starch/carbs.

Per bowl   400 calories • 12 g fat • 19 g carbs • 5 g fiber • 48 g protein

Nourishment Breakdown

PROTEIN salmon, edamame	**FIBER** cabbage, cucumber, edamame	**CARB/STARCH** edamame
FAT salmon, edamame		

Sloppy Joe Power Bowls

Easy to prep ahead of time and it's fun to build your own bowl for dinner. You can make the sloppy Joe mixture and put it in a salad or wrap for a quick dinner. My kids love them on hamburger buns with cheese on top and with potatoes or microwaved instant rice on the side. The protein, fiber, and fat will make you feel full and keep late-night cravings away.

1 onion, chopped

1 green bell pepper, chopped

2 pounds (900 g) lean ground beef or turkey

1 cup (107 g) frozen riced cauliflower

6 ounces (195 g) tomato paste

2 tablespoons (22 g) yellow mustard

2 tablespoons (30 ml) coconut aminos

1 tablespoon (7 g) chili powder

1 teaspoon garlic powder

½ teaspoon salt

¼ teaspoon pepper

Quick Slaw (page 159)

Marinated Mushrooms (page 140)

In a large skillet over medium heat, brown onion and bell pepper until softened and fragrant.

Add meat and cook through, drain fat if needed.

Add riced cauliflower and remaining ingredients. Stir and cook on low for 5 minutes or until all combined.

Next, prepare Quick Slaw and Marinated Mushrooms.

To assemble bowls as a meal prep, start with 5 containers. Add 1½ cups (340 g) slaw, ½ cup (35 g) mushrooms, and 1½ cups (312 g) meat mixture to each container.

Per bowl with slaw and mushrooms

345 calories • 145 g fat • 20 g carbs • 7 g fiber • 43 g protein

Nourishment Breakdown

PROTEIN meat	**FIBER** slaw, cauliflower,	**CARB/STARCH** none
FAT meat, cheese	mushrooms, onion,	unless add bun,
	bell pepper	potatoes, or rice

Carnitas Power Bowls

5 BOWLS

Super easy to prep for the week or prepare the ingredients and put them in a slow cooker for dinner. The corn salad is loaded with flavor and fresh herbs like cilantro which helps rid the body of heavy metals and lowers blood sugar levels. Add it to dishes when you can.

MEAT

1.5 pounds (672 g) pork or turkey tenderloins, about 2

16 ounces (500 g) salsa

3 cloves garlic, minced

2 tablespoons (15 g) taco seasoning

¼ cup (60 ml) coconut aminos

¼ cup (60 ml) lime juice

CORN SALAD

15 ounces (322 g) black beans, drained and rinsed

15 ounces (330 g) canned corn, drained

½ cup (80 g) red onion, diced

2 tablespoons (30 ml) apple cider vinegar or white vinegar

½ teaspoon cumin

½ teaspoon chili powder

⅓ cup (5 g) fresh cilantro, chopped

⅓ cup (50 g) Cotija or feta cheese, crumbled

OPTIONAL ADD-INS

Greek yogurt or sour cream

Lettuce

Cauliflower rice

TO MAKE THE MEAT

Place tenderloins in a slow cooker and add salsa, garlic, taco seasoning, aminos, and lime juice.

Cook on low for 4 to 5 hours or high for 3 hours.

Shred meat after it's done cooking and place back in the slow cooker.

TO MAKE THE CORN SALAD

In a large bowl, add all corn salad ingredients and stir well.

TO ASSEMBLE

Add 1 cup (175 g) of corn salad and ¾ cup (132 g) of the carnitas meat mixture to containers. Top with Greek yogurt or sour cream if desired.

Per bowl with pork

402 calories • 85 g fat • 31 g carbs • 5 g fiber • 43 g protein

Per bowl with turkey

310 calories • 4 g fat • 35 g carbs • 5 g fiber • 34 g protein

Nourishment Breakdown

PROTEIN turkey/pork	**FIBER** onion, cilantro, some in beans
FAT cheese, pork	**CARB/STARCH** beans, corn

Burger Power Bowls

This simple recipe is easy to prep ahead of time for a family dinner. Each member can fix their bowl the way they want it thanks to a variety of toppings and additions. You can keep it simple with toppings or do them all, but either way, you'll be eating a balanced meal.

MEAT

2 pounds (900 g) lean ground beef

½ teaspoon garlic powder

½ teaspoon onion powder

½ teaspoon pepper

1 tablespoon (11 g)
yellow mustard

1 tablespoon (15 ml) coconut
aminos or Worcestershire
sauce

BURGER SAUCE

⅓ cup (77 g) nonfat Greek
yogurt or avocado mayo

2 tablespoons (30 g)
unsweetened ketchup

2 teaspoons yellow mustard

2 tablespoons (30 g) dill pickle
relish, or grate or chop pickles

1 tablespoon (15 ml) pickle juice
or white vinegar

¼ teaspoon pepper

½ teaspoon salt

½ teaspoon paprika

BOWL BASE AND TOPPINGS

(optional, add what you like)

16 ounces (144 g) mushrooms
or the Marinated Mushrooms
(page 140)

Red or white onion, sliced (raw)
or Caramelized Onions
(page 141)

2 heads of lettuce or 4 romaine
hearts, chopped (2 bags of
salad works too)

10 ounces (190 g) grape
tomatoes, sliced in half

½ cup (58 g) cheddar cheese,
shredded

Pickle chips or wedges

Fresh dill

TO MAKE THE MEAT

In a large skillet over medium heat, brown ground beef and
strain off any fat.

Return meat to skillet and add all other meat ingredients.

Turn to low heat, stirring occasionally.

TO MAKE THE BURGER SAUCE

While that's cooking, make your burger sauce by combining all
of the sauce ingredients in a small bowl. Stir well and set aside.

Next, prepare the Marinated Mushrooms and Caramelized
Onions, if desired.

TO ASSEMBLE

Assemble by adding to each bowl about 1½ cups (83 g) of
lettuce, 1 cup (224 g) meat mixture, ½ cup (35 g) each of mushrooms and onions, 4 to 5 grape tomatoes, 2 tablespoons (8 g)
cheese, desired sliced pickles, fresh dill, and 2 tablespoons (32 g)
of burger sauce.

Per bowl with all the fixings

345 calories • 13 g fat • 10 g carbs • 2 g fiber • 46 g protein

Nourishment Breakdown

PROTEIN beef, Greek yogurt	**FIBER** veggies
FAT some in beef, cheese, mayo if using	**CARB/STARCH** none

9

Warm Veggie Sides

NONSTARCHY VEGETABLES are important in managing blood sugar because they're typically lower in carbs and have a low glycemic index. The glycemic index is a scale to measure how fast and how much foods can raise blood sugar levels.

The fiber in vegetables helps to slow down the digestion and absorption of carbs, which prevents rapid spikes in blood sugar. Some vegetables contain compounds that may improve insulin sensitivity. Veggies also usually are higher in fiber and contain essential vitamins, minerals, and antioxidants.

Veggies can be eaten at a higher volume if you're looking for satiety without a crazy high calorie load. Keep in mind that these are moderate fat recipes, so don't be afraid to add them to your plate on a regular basis. Use these fiber-rich vegetable recipes to complement the protein, fat, and carb components of meals for optimal blood sugar balance.

Marinated Mushrooms

This dish is yummy as a burger or steak topping, in a burger, or added to Sloppy Joe power bowls. Mushrooms are always an easy and super flavorful veggie.

16 ounces (144 g) sliced baby Bella mushrooms (or any you prefer)

3 tablespoons (45 ml) coconut aminos

3 tablespoons (45 ml) balsamic vinegar

½ teaspoon pepper

Place sliced mushrooms in a sprayed large skillet over medium heat and add other ingredients.

Cook for 5 to 10 minutes, stirring occasionally. If you cook them longer, the marinade will be more flavorful.

Per serving   15 calories • 0 g fat • 3 g carbs • 1 g fiber • 1 g protein

Nourishment Breakdown

PROTEIN none

FAT none

FIBER mushrooms

CARB/STARCH none

Caramelized Onions

Choose these caramelized onions as the perfect topper or side for burger or taco night. They're a yummy addition to a salad too. They're super light with no added oil, so you can enjoy a flavorful veggie that's full of fiber which helps slow digestion. That's especially important for your blood sugar if you follow up that burger or taco with sweets.

3 white onions, sliced thin

½ teaspoon pepper

2 tablespoons (30 ml) balsamic vinegar

2 tablespoons (30 ml) coconut aminos

In a large sprayed skillet, over medium heat. Place onions and all other ingredients.

Cook for 5 to 10 minutes, stirring occasionally until desired tenderness is achieved. The longer they cook, they will get more caramelized.

Per serving   23 calories • 5 g carbs • 1 g fiber • 5 g protein

Nourishment Breakdown

PROTEIN none

FAT none

FIBER onion

CARB/STARCH none

Roasted Broccoli

There's something about the lemon-garlic combination in this recipe. It tastes buttery but without any butter! It's light and delicious and makes for easy leftovers to add to salads, egg scrambles, or with any protein for a quick balanced meal. Just allow the broccoli to cool before storing in the fridge so it doesn't become soggy.

24 ounces (312 g) chopped broccoli florets, or 3 heads, chopped

1 teaspoon garlic powder (or 1 clove, minced, or ½ teaspoon everything but the bagel seasoning)

½ teaspoon salt (if not using seasoning)

1 lemon, juiced

Preheat to 400°F (200°C, or gas mark 6).

Place chopped broccoli in a single layer on a lined sheet pan.

Spray broccoli with olive oil or avocado oil and season with spices.

Bake for 20 to 25 minutes. Remove from oven and add lemon juice evenly over the cooked broccoli.

Per serving   30 calories • 0 g fat • 6 g carbs • 2 g fiber • 2 g protein

Nourishment Breakdown

PROTEIN none

FAT none

FIBER broccoli

CARB/STARCH none

Crispy Brussels Sprouts

Pair this nourishing veggie with protein found in chicken, steak, or fish. You'll also get protein from the Canadian bacon which adds some crunch. Flavorful and light and a good fiber source for your plate.

24 ounces (176 g) Brussels sprouts, trimmed and halved

4 slices uncured Canadian bacon, chopped into small pieces

2 tablespoons (30 ml) balsamic vinegar

½ teaspoon salt

¼ teaspoon pepper

¼ cup (25 g) shaved or shredded Parmesan

Preheat oven to 425°F (220°C or gas mark 7).

Place Brussels sprouts in a single layer on a lined baking sheet. Spray with avocado or olive oil.

Add all other ingredients in the order listed evenly over the top of the Brussels sprouts.

Bake for 20 to 25 minutes. Switch to high broil for 2 to 3 additional minutes to make crispy. Watch them carefully because they burn easily on broil.

Per serving   67 calories • 1 g fat • 5 g carbs • 2 g fiber • 5 g protein

Nourishment Breakdown

PROTEIN small amount in bacon and cheese
FAT small amount in cheese

FIBER Brussels
CARB/STARCH none

Parmesan Asparagus

This veggie side dish is delish, super light, and adds fiber to your plate. Parmesan is a robust cheese and adds flavor along with fat. This super simple recipe is ready in 15 minutes.

1 pound (268 g) fresh asparagus, wood ends removed
1 teaspoon garlic powder or
   1 clove garlic, minced
½ teaspoon salt
¼ teaspoon pepper
¼ cup (25 g) grated or shredded Parmesan cheese

Preheat oven to 400°F (200°C, or gas mark 6).

Place asparagus stalks on a lined or sprayed sheet pan.

Season with seasonings and top with Parmesan cheese.

Bake for 10 to 15 minutes. Switch to high broil and cook 2 to 3 more minutes to brown the cheese, if desired.

Per serving   34 calories • 1 g fat • 3 g carbs • 1 g fiber • 3 g protein

Nourishment Breakdown

PROTEIN	small amount in cheese	**FIBER**	asparagus
FAT	cheese	**CARB/STARCH**	none

Glazed Thyme Carrots

Delicious and a reliable fiber source for your optimal plate balance along with protein, fat and carbs. We love eating these as part of a weeknight dinner. This dish is also a great addition to any holiday table. Veggies don't need to be doused in fat and sugar to taste good when they're cooked properly. (Pictured on page 138.)

2 pounds (908 g) whole carrots

2 tablespoons (30 ml) coconut aminos

½ teaspoon salt

¼ teaspoon pepper

2 teaspoon fresh chopped thyme (or ½ teaspoon dried), plus more for garnish when serving

Preheat oven to 400°F (200°C, or gas mark 6).

Wash carrots well. I don't scrape or peel them, but it's up to you. Cut thicker carrots in half lengthwise and chop into desired size. You want the pieces similar in size to evenly cook.

Place carrots on a lined sheet pan. Spray carrots with olive or avocado oil, pour aminos over carrots, and add spices.

Bake for 25 to 30 minutes. If you're going for extra glazing, switch oven to high broil and cook an additional 2 to 4 minutes longer. You'll need to watch them though because they'll burn. Garnish them with fresh thyme for a nice added touch.

Per serving   38 calories • 0 g fat • 9 g carbs • 2 g fiber • 1 g protein

Nourishment Breakdown

PROTEIN none

FAT none

FIBER carrots

CARB/STARCH none

Warm Veggie Sides

10

Fancy Salads

SALADS HAVE A LOW glycemic index and are full of dietary fiber which can slow down the digestion and absorption of carbs. This reduces the rate at which glucose enters the blood stream and can help with blood sugar control. Salads are also packed with vitamins, minerals, and lots of helpful antioxidants. It's a great way to fit in a lot of nutrition in a tasty, feel-good way.

All these salad recipes just need a protein source to make them a meal. Add a rotisserie chicken or grilled shrimp and you're all set. These salads also make a great option if you need to bring a dish to a party or a get-together. That way you know you'll have a healthy option and a balanced plate. The dressings are all light and don't add much fat, so fatty fish or steak can still be a protein choice.

Antipasto Chickpea Salad

I love to bring this flavorful dish to a cookout or an any time of the year party. We like it best served over chopped romaine lettuce or cooked spaghetti squash boats. It reminds me of a supreme pizza, but I feel great after eating it thanks to the protein, fiber, and fat it contains. It contains a wide array of nutrients that nourish the body and help to maintain stable blood glucose levels.

Two 15-ounce (450-g) cans of
    chickpeas, rinsed and drained

½ cup (50 g) sliced kalamata
    olives

½ cup (75 g) jarred roasted red
    bell peppers, chopped

½ cup (68 g) jarred sliced
    pepperoncini peppers,
    desired heat

14 ounces (525 g) canned
    artichoke hearts (in water,
    not oil), drained and chopped

4 ounces (112 g) uncured turkey
    pepperoni, sliced

2 ounces (56 g) prosciutto,
    chopped

½ cup (75 g) feta cheese,
    crumbled

¼ cup (10 g) fresh basil,
    chopped

¼ cup (60 ml) red wine vinegar

1 lemon, juiced

½ teaspoon Italian seasoning

¼ teaspoon pepper

1 tablespoon (11 g) Dijon
    mustard

In a large bowl, add all ingredients and stir well.

Serve cold over romaine lettuce for a salad or as a side dish.

Per serving   348 calories • 15 g fat • 31 g carbs • 7 g fiber • 19 g protein

Nourishment Breakdown

PROTEIN pepperoni, prosciutto, chickpeas

FAT cheese, olives, pepperoni, prosciutto

FIBER veggies

CARB/STARCH chickpeas

Kale Crunch Salad

This salad is a favorite for any season of the year. There's a little crunch in each bite from the celery and almonds and a creamy, dreamy dressing that's loaded with flavor. I always get asked for this salad recipe when I bring it to a get-together. Just add a protein source, and you've got a simple, blood sugar balanced meal.

SALAD

8 ounces (67 g) baby kale

10 ounces (284 g) slaw mix

½ cup (75 g) fresh blueberries

3 celery stalks, chopped

¼ cup (40 g) red onion or Quick
    Pickled Onion (page 160)

¼ cup (25 g) shredded or
    shaved Parmesan

¼ cup (28 g) sliced almonds

DRESSING

1 cup (225 g) low-fat cottage
    cheese

¼ cup (60 ml) almond milk

3 cloves garlic, minced

½ lemon, juiced

¼ cup (25 g) shredded or
    shaved Parmesan

1 tablespoon (15 ml) apple
    cider vinegar

1 tablespoon (11 g) Dijon or
    spicy brown mustard

1 tablespoon (15 ml) coconut
    aminos or Worcestershire
    sauce

½ teaspoon salt

¼ teaspoon pepper

In a large salad bowl, add all salad ingredients and set aside.

To make the dressing, add all dressing ingredients to a blender or food processor and blend until smooth.

Pour salad dressing over salad and toss.

Per serving   166 calories • 6 g fat • 15 g carbs • 6 g fiber • 11 g protein

Nourishment Breakdown

PROTEIN some in cottage cheese

FAT Parmesan, almonds

FIBER kale, slaw, celery, onion

CARB/STARCH some in blueberries

Crunchy Mandarin Salad

I love this salad with any protein, but grilled steak is my favorite. It's also a crowd pleaser so you can use it as your go-to dish for get-togethers and parties. The mandarins and clementines add color and vitamin C, which boosts immunity so it's a perfect dish for summer or winter as cold season rolls around.

SALAD

10 ounces (40 g) spring
    mix greens

⅓ cup (48 g) peanuts

3 mandarins or clementines,
    segmented

1 apple, sliced thin

1 bunch green onions,
    chopped small (white and
    light green part)

⅓ cup (50 g) feta or goat
    cheese, crumbled

ORANGE VINAIGRETTE DRESSING

2 tablespoons (30 ml) olive oil

¼ cup (60 ml) rice vinegar

2 tablespoons (28 ml) fresh
    orange juice (½ an orange)

1 tablespoon (11 g) Dijon or
    brown mustard

½ teaspoon salt

½ teaspoon pepper

2 tablespoons (30 ml) water,
    optional

In a large bowl combine all salad ingredients.

Add dressing ingredients to a jar with a lid and shake well to mix. Add water if thinner consistency desired.

Pour dressing over salad and toss.

Per serving   132 calories • 9 g fat • 10 g carbs • 2 g fiber • 4 g protein

Nourishment Breakdown

PROTEIN none

FAT peanuts, oil, cheese

FIBER greens, onion

CARB/STARCH mandarins, apple

Fancy Salads

Strawberry Spinach Salad

This salad is so flavorful and light—it tastes like summer thanks to fresh mint and berries. It's also delish in the winter and looks pretty on any holiday table. Add any protein source, like a rotisserie chicken or grilled fish or meat, and you've got a complete balanced meal to keep your tank full and your energy humming.

SALAD

10 ounces (40 g) fresh
  baby spinach

1 pound (290 g) fresh
  strawberries, chopped

⅓ cup (37 g) pecan halves
  or pieces

1 shallot, sliced thin

4 fresh mint leaves, chopped
  small

¼ cup (38 g) feta or goat
  cheese, crumbled

DRESSING

¼ cup (60 ml) balsamic vinegar

2 tablespoons (30 ml) olive oil

2 tablespoons (30 ml) water

1 tablespoon (11 g) poppy seeds
  or chia seeds

2 tablespoons (16 g)
  sesame seeds

1 teaspoon Dijon mustard

½ teaspoon coconut aminos or
  Worcestershire sauce

¼ teaspoon pepper

¼ teaspoon salt

Add all salad ingredients to a large bowl.

To a covered jar, add dressing ingredients. Cover and shake well.

Pour over salad and toss.

Per serving   128 calories • 7 g fat • 11 g carbs • 4 g fiber • 2 g protein

Nourishment Breakdown

PROTEIN none

FAT pecans, cheese, oil

FIBER spinach, shallot

CARB/STARCH strawberries

Fancy Salads

Gorgonzola Pear Salad

This salad tastes like fall, and you'll love the spiced candied pecans. Add any protein source like a rotisserie chicken or canned tuna if you don't want to cook and you've got a complete blood sugar balanced meal. I often bring this dish to holiday gatherings and it's always a crowd pleaser. The fiber in the salad acts as a buffer to slow blood sugar absorption from any extra carbs I might indulge in.

PECANS

1 tablespoon (14 g) butter

1 tablespoon (16 g) granulated
   monk fruit or desired
   sweetener (allulose and
   stevia are other natural
   options)

1 teaspoon cinnamon

⅓ cup (37 g) pecan halves

SALAD

10 ounces (69 g) spring mix
   salad greens

1 pear, ripe and thinly sliced

¼ cup (30 g) Gorgonzola,
   crumbled

THYME VINAIGRETTE DRESSING

¼ cup (60 ml) white
   wine vinegar

2 tablespoons (30 ml) olive oil

2 tablespoons (30 ml) water

1 tablespoon (11 g) Dijon
   mustard

½ teaspoon salt

¼ teaspoon pepper

½ shallot, chopped

1 teaspoon fresh thyme,
   chopped

1 lemon, juiced

In a skillet over low heat, add butter, monk fruit or sweetener, and cinnamon until melted. Place pecans in mixture and toss/stir until coated. Remove the pan from the heat and set aside to cook.

In a large salad bowl, add greens, pear, cheese, and candied pecans.

Chop the thyme and shallot into small pieces.

Put the dressing ingredients in a jar and shake to combine or put into a blender or food processor and blend until smooth.

Add all dressing to salad, toss, and enjoy!

Per serving   147 calories • 10 g fat • 12 g carbs • 5 g fiber • 3 g protein

Nourishment Breakdown

PROTEIN not much, add a
protein source
FAT pecans, butter, oil

FIBER greens, some in pear
CARB/STARCH pear

Cucumber Vinegar Salad

This salad is refreshing and light and tastes like summer, especially when you can add fresh tomatoes in season. Serve it on its own or as an appetizer. It's perfect for any occasion, from a cook-out to a gathering any time of the year. This salad also contains lots of fiber to slow digestion, so it's a good choice if you plan to eat a carb or starch with your meal to prevent sugar spikes.

2 long English cucumbers, sliced thin

½ red onion, sliced thin

½ teaspoon Italian seasoning

¼ teaspoon salt

¼ teaspoon pepper

1 lemon, juiced

3 tablespoons (45 ml) balsamic vinegar, white vinegar works too

¼ cup (38 g) crumbled feta

In a large bowl combine all ingredients and toss to combine.

This can be made ahead of time and stored in the fridge.

Per serving   34 calories • 5 g fat • 6 g carbs • 5 g fiber • 1 g protein

Nourishment Breakdown

PROTEIN none

FAT none

FIBER cucumber, onion

CARB/STARCH none

Quick Slaw

This versatile recipe can be used as part of a power bowl along with a protein, as a taco topper, or as a side dish. It contains plenty of fiber from vegetables to slow down digestion, especially if you follow it with a carb or starch which can affect blood sugar levels. I often prepare this dish for barbecues in the summer and as a side dish if I'm grilling food outside. Prep a batch and place it in the fridge so that it's ready when you need it.

1 bag coleslaw mix

¼ cup (60 g) avocado mayo or nonfat Greek yogurt (or a mixture of the two)

1 tablespoon (11 g) Dijon mustard, optional

2 tablespoons (30 ml) apple cider vinegar

½ teaspoon salt

½ teaspoon pepper

¼ cup (38 g) feta cheese

Add all ingredients to a bowl and stir.

Great to make ahead and allow to soften a few hours in the fridge. Good for 4 days in the fridge.

Per serving with nonfat Greek yogurt

58 calories • 15 g fat • 5 g carbs • 2 g fiber • 4 g protein

Nourishment Breakdown

PROTEIN none, pair with protein
FAT mayo, cheese (if adding)

FIBER cabbage
CARB/STARCH none

FLAVOR SWAPS

MEXICAN 1 teaspoon cumin, ¼ cup (4 g) cilantro chopped, ½ red onion chopped, 1 lime juiced, skip the Dijon, swap feta for Cotija cheese

ASIAN 1 teaspoon ginger, ¼ cup (60 ml) rice vinegar, 1 tablespoon (15 ml) coconut aminos, ½ scallion chopped, skip the Dijon, ¼ cup (35 g) peanuts chopped, optional

Fancy Salads

Quick Pickled Onions

Pickled onions "count" as fiber in your meal and are so good in or on tacos, salads, eggs, toast, or soup. The color of the dish also brightens any table. When I can, I prep these so I can add them to any meal I choose. It's that good!

1 large or 2 small red onions, sliced thin

⅓ cup (75 ml) apple cider vinegar

½ teaspoon salt

¼ teaspoon pepper

½ teaspoon garlic powder, optional

1 lemon, juiced

Hot water

Place all ingredients in a jar and cover onions with hot water to just cover. Store in fridge.

Good for up to a week, but ours never lasts that long. I usually use an 18-ounce (532-ml) canning jar.

Per serving   16 calories • 0 g fat • 3carbs • 1 g fiber • 1 g protein

Nourishment Breakdown

PROTEIN none

FAT none

FIBER onion

CARB/STARCH none

Green Goddess Salad

This salad is refreshing and light. It's yummy as a dip with tortilla chips too. Pair with a protein source, and you've got a complete meal to keep your blood sugar balanced. I love to add lemon to spinach when I can because it aids in iron absorption.

8 ounces (55 g) shredded iceberg lettuce

10 ounces (284 g) angel hair coleslaw

1 cup (120 g) cucumbers, diced small

1 bundle green onions, chopped small

DRESSING

1 cup (30 g) fresh spinach

½ cup (20 g) fresh basil

2 cloves garlic, minced

1 small shallot, chopped

2 tablespoons (6 g) chives

2 lemons, juiced

½ cup (25 g) grated Parmesan

2 tablespoons (30 ml) olive oil

2 tablespoons (30 ml) rice vinegar

2 tablespoons (30 ml) water, if needed to thin

1 teaspoon salt

Add lettuce, slaw, cucumbers, and green onions to a large salad bowl.

In a blender or food processor, add all dressing ingredients and blend well.

Pour dressing over salad and toss well. Enjoy!

Per serving 127 calories • 8 g fat • 8 g carbs • 2 g fiber • 4 g protein

Nourishment Breakdown

PROTEIN small amount in cheese

FAT cheese, oil

FIBER all the veggies

CARB/STARCH none

Balanced Desserts

A HEALTHY DESSERT can satisfy your sweet tooth, provide nutrients, and minimize added sugars and unhealthy fats too. These balanced desserts are blood sugar friendly because they don't contain maple syrup, dates, or honey. While those are natural occurring sweeteners, they still affect blood sugar in a similar way to any sugar. Instead, choose natural sweeteners like monk fruit, allulose, and stevia. Cooked this way, these desserts fit well into a balanced blood sugar diet. They're delicious, satisfying, and will still help you reach your health and wellness goals.

Chocolate Protein Pudding

This pudding is a great balanced sweet-tooth fix that can be prepped ahead of time. It's perfect for a dinner party too, and trust me, nobody will know that it's tofu. Dark chocolate is the bonus here, since it contains flavonoids, which are plant compounds that act as antioxidants. This recipe contains fat, starch, and protein so it's a blood sugar friendly treat after dinner or when eaten as a snack.

¼ cup (70 g) dark chocolate, melted

16 ounces (454 g) silken tofu, organic if possible

Dash of salt

2 tablespoons (10 g) cacao powder

½ cup (64 g) chocolate protein powder

Melt chocolate over a double boiler or in a glass bowl in the microwave for 1 minute and stir until fully melted.

Add all ingredients to a blender and blend until creamy. Mine took 1 minute on low.

Pour into 4 ramekins or 3 tea cups.

Refrigerate a few hours or overnight to set. Good for a week in the refrigerator.

Per serving in ramekins 170 calories • 7 g fat • 75 g carbs • 15 g protein

Per serving in tea cups 220 calories • 9 g fat • 10 g carbs • 20 g protein

Nourishment Breakdown

PROTEIN tofu, protein powder
FAT tofu, dark chocolate
FIBER none

CARB/STARCH small amount in chocolate, can add berries as a topping if desired

Single-Serve Chocolate Cookie

I eat my cookie with Greek yogurt or cottage cheese because I feel my best with at least 30 g protein per meal to keep me in my healthy blood sugar range. It also contains fat, fiber, and carbs. You can prep this yummy treat ahead of time, cooked or uncooked, and store it in the fridge.

¼ cup (39 g) oats or
    2 tablespoons (12 g)
    coconut flour

⅓ cup (43 g) chocolate
    protein powder

Dash of salt

½ teaspoon vanilla extract

1 tablespoon (16 g) almond
    or peanut butter

1 tablespoon (15 ml) milk
    of choice

Desired dark chocolate chips
    (I used about 10)

Preheat oven to 350°F (180°C, or gas mark 4).

Combine ingredients (except chocolate chips) in a small bowl.

Stir well. It will be crumbly but add more milk if needed (protein powders can vary).

Shape into a cookie shape on a lined baking sheet. Top with chocolate chips.

Bake for 7 to 8 minutes in the oven or air fryer at 350°F (180°C) for 3 to 4 minutes. You can also microwave for 1½ minutes in the bowl, but you'll have to eat it with a spoon.

Allow to cool 5 minutes or so to harden.

Per cookie with oats

315 calories • 12 g fat • 22 g carbs • 4 g fiber • 27 g protein

Per cookie with coconut flour

300 calories • 145 g fat • 18 g carbs • 7 g fiber • 27 g protein

Nourishment Breakdown

PROTEIN powder	**FIBER** none
FAT nut butter, dark chocolate	**CARB/STARCH** oats

No-Bake Buckeyes

A light, anytime dessert. This recipe contains 9 grams of protein per ball. Perfect if you're a chocolate and peanut butter fan. I confess that I make the real-deal, sugar-laden recipe for the holidays, but this version which contains protein, fat, fiber, and a carb source is much better for blood sugar balance. It satisfies that sweet tooth without the spike.

1 cup (245 g) unsweetened applesauce

1 teaspoon vanilla extract

⅓ cup (43 g) vanilla protein powder

⅓ cup (52 g) oats (can be gluten-free if needed)

⅔ cup (85 g) peanut butter powder

⅓ cup (30 g) coconut flour

⅓ cup (58 g) dark chocolate chips

In a medium bowl combine all ingredients except chocolate chips. Stir well.

Form the wet dough into 2-inch (5-cm) balls and place on a lined cookie sheet. Put into the fridge to set.

In a small glass bowl, melt the chocolate chips. Allow 1½ minutes in the microwave. If heated for more time, it'll ruin the texture. They may still be in morsel shape so stir until smooth without overheating. You can also heat this ingredient on a low setting on the stovetop.

Once melted, dip each ball into chocolate to cover halfway. Store in the fridge or freezer. We like them frozen. Good for a week in the fridge.

Per ball   97 calories • 25 g fat • 11 g carbs • 4 g fiber • 9 g protein

Nourishment Breakdown

PROTEIN powder, peanut butter powder

FAT dark chocolate

FIBER coconut flour, peanut butter powder

CARB/STARCH oats, applesauce

Birthday Cake Energy Bites

This easy no-bake recipe is a no-brainer for a quick snack that satisfies. I often double the recipe since I'm getting my hands messy already. Butter extract will also help give it that batter flavor. Ingredients including almond or cashew butter, protein powder, and fiber from oats make this snack blood sugar friendly.

½ cup (130 g) almond or cashew butter

¼ cup (32 g) vanilla protein powder

⅓ cup (30 g) coconut flour

¼ cup (39 g) oats

1 teaspoon cake batter extract

¼ cup (60 ml) almond or coconut milk

¼ teaspoon pink salt

Desired sprinkles, optional

In a medium bowl, add all ingredients except sprinkles. Mix with hands to combine.

Add sprinkles, and a splash more milk if too dry to form balls. Texture and thickness can depend on the type of protein powder used. Store in the fridge up to a week.

Per ball   110 calories • 7 g fat • 5 g carbs • 2 g fiber • 5 g protein

Nourishment Breakdown

PROTEIN powder

FAT nut butter

FIBER coconut flour, oats

CARB/STARCH oats

Vanilla Sheet Cake

This light-as-a-feather cake is a hit any time of the year. I like to add berries to the top especially on the Fourth of July and you can also make it festive with sprinkles for the holidays or any celebration. For plate balance, this contains healthy fats, and you can also add fruit for fiber to slow absorption of the carbs. No one will guess that it's blood sugar friendly!

1 cup (112 g) almond flour

¾ cup (68 g) coconut flour

2 teaspoons baking soda

¼ teaspoon salt

3 eggs

¼ cup (55 g) butter, softened

½ cup (125 g) unsweetened applesauce

1 cup (230 g) nonfat Greek yogurt

¼ cup (60 ml) almond milk

1 teaspoon vanilla extract

½ cup (125 g) unsweetened applesauce

1 cup (240 g) granulated sweetener (I used monk fruit/erythritol blend; Allulose or stevia works well too but is more concentrated so use a smaller amount

Preheat oven to 325°F (170°C, or gas mark 3).

In a large bowl, add flours, baking soda, and salt. Stir to combine and set aside.

In a large mixing bowl, add eggs, softened butter, applesauce, yogurt, milk, and vanilla extract. Mix with a mixer on low until well combined. Add granulated sweetener and mix on low/medium until combined. Add flour mixture and mix until all blended.

Pour into a greased 9 x 13-inch (23 x 33-cm) glass dish and bake for 45 to 50 minutes.

While baking, make Cream Cheese Icing.

Once your cake has cooled, add icing. Slice into 12 square pieces and store in the fridge, covered. Good for a week.

Per serving   204 calories • 15 g fat • 8 g carbs • 4 g fiber • 6 g protein

Nourishment Breakdown

PROTEIN some in flours, yogurt, eggs

FAT egg yolks, almond flour, butter

FIBER coconut flour, applesauce

CARB/STARCH applesauce

Cream Cheese Icing

8 ounces (225 g) ⅓-less fat cream cheese, softened

½ teaspoon vanilla extract

¼ cup (32 g) confectioners' sugar replacement

In a glass bowl, microwave cream cheese 30 seconds to soften.

Add vanilla and sweetener and mix with a mixer until desired icing consistency is achieved, usually 2 minutes.

Flourless Protein Brownies

These are super easy to prep ahead of time for the week. I usually double the recipe and freeze half. Right out of the freezer they have a delish ice cream sandwich texture. I find using canned sweet potatoes makes it super easy to whip up a batch. Keep in mind that the type of protein powder, or whether it's plant-based or vegan, can affect the texture, so experiment a bit to find what you like best. Since this dessert contains protein, fat, and carbs, you'll feel full and satisfy your sweet tooth.

WET INGREDIENTS

1 cup (245 g) cooked or canned
   sweet potato or pumpkin

½ cup (130 g) natural almond
   or peanut butter

1 egg or flax egg

½ cup (120 ml) water or milk

1 teaspoon vanilla extract

DRY INGREDIENTS

¼ cup (22 g) cacao or
   unsweetened cocoa powder

3 tablespoons (24 g) granulated
   monk fruit or allulose
   sweetener blend

¼ cup (32 g) vanilla or
   chocolate protein powder

1 teaspoon baking soda

¼ teaspoon salt

⅓ cup (58 g) dark
   chocolate chips

Preheat oven to 350°F (180°C, or gas mark 4).

Mash the potatoes (or pumpkin), nut butter, egg/flax egg, water/milk, and vanilla extract. Stir well.

Add all remaining ingredients except chocolate chips. Stir to combine. Add chips.

Pour batter into an 8 x 8-inch (20 x 20-cm) pan and bake for 25 to 30 minutes. Store in the fridge. Good for up to a week. If doubling the recipe, bake in a 9 x 13-inch (23 x 33-cm) dish and cook 35 to 40 minutes

---

Per serving   156 calories • 8 g fat • 9 g carbs • 4 g fiber • 11 g protein

Nourishment Breakdown

PROTEIN powder
FAT nut butter, dark chocolate, flax if using

FIBER some in potato/pumpkin
CARB/STARCH potato/pumpkin

Chocolate Ganache Cake

I usually make this for my dad's birthday. Everyone, even the teenage boys who attend the party, all say it tastes like "regular" chocolate cake. What they don't know is that it contains plenty of healthy fats and nourishing ingredients, but the sugar content is low. It's the perfect dessert after a lean protein meal to stay in balance.

DRY INGREDIENTS

2 cups (224 g) almond flour

½ cup (45 g) coconut flour

1 cup (86 g) cacao powder

1 cup (128 g) granulated monk fruit or allulose blend. Stevia is a great natural sweetener but use a smaller amount because it's more concentrated

2 tablespoons (10 g) instant coffee grounds, optional for a richer taste

½ teaspoon salt

2 teaspoon baking soda

WET INGREDIENTS

1 ripe avocado

1 cup (245 g) cooked or canned sweet potato or pumpkin

1 cup (230 g) nonfat Greek yogurt (or dairy-free Greek yogurt)

1 cup (235 ml) almond milk

2 eggs (or 4 vegan eggs)

¼ cup (60 ml) liquid egg whites

2 teaspoons vanilla extract

Preheat oven to 350°F (180°C, or gas mark 4).

Add all the dry ingredients to a bowl and stir. Set aside.

With a mixer combine all the wet ingredients. Slowly add dry mixture and mix with mixer for 1 minute or so until combined.

Pour batter into two 8-inch (20-cm) greased and floured rounds and bake for 35 to 45 minutes. Mine usually take 35 minutes.

Allow to cool before removing from pan. You can also make cupcakes which take about 20 to 25 minutes to bake or make a sheet cake in a 9 x 13-inch (23 x 33-cm) glass dish (it's the easiest way to me) by baking for 35 to 40 minutes.

When I use 2 round cake pans, I use store-bought low-sugar chocolate icing for the middle layer and ganache for the top. I use the icing for the cupcakes and the 9 x 13-inch (23 x 33-cm) cake.

Pour over cooled cake and immediately put in fridge to store. You can also heat slowly over low heat while stirring on the stove top.

Per serving   356 calories • 23 g fat • 26 g carbs • 10 g fiber • 10 g protein

Nourishment Breakdown

PROTEIN a little in yogurt
FAT avocado, almond flour, yolks, ganache

FIBER coconut flour, some in avocado
CARB/STARCH sweet potato

Ganache Icing

1½ cups (262 g) dark chocolate, chips or bar

½ cup (115 g) coconut cream (do not shake—you'll use the stuff at the top of the can)

Microwave both ingredients for 30 seconds in a glass bowl, stir well and cook 30 more seconds, if needed.

Peanut Butter Blondie Muffins

This tasty recipe is always popular. It's a balanced snack or dessert because it contains protein, fat, fiber, and carbs. Canned sweet potato and canned pumpkin make this recipe easy to put together but check for added sugar.

WET INGREDIENTS

2 cups (490 g) cooked or canned sweet potato or pumpkin

2 eggs or ⅓ cup (73 g) whites

1 cup (235 ml) almond, coconut milk, or water

2 teaspoons vanilla extract

⅔ cup (172 g) peanut butter (natural or organic with peanuts and salt as only ingredients)

DRY INGREDIENTS

½ cup (64 g) vanilla protein powder

½ cup (45 g) coconut flour

2 teaspoons baking powder

⅓ cup (43 g) granulated monk fruit or allulose sweetener blend

¼ teaspoon pink salt

½ cup (87 g) dark chocolate chips of choice

Preheat oven to 350°F (180°C, or gas mark 4).

Mash sweet potatoes (or pumpkin) with potato masher, add all other wet ingredients. Stir well.

Add all dry ingredients except chocolate chips, stir. Add chips and stir again.

Scoop batter with a ⅓-cup measuring cup (38 g) into a lined muffin pan. Bake at for 25 to 30 minutes. For blondie squares, use a sprayed 9 x 13-inch (23 x 33-cm) dish and bake for 35 to 40 minutes. Allow to cool before cutting. Store in the fridge. Good for a week either way.

Per blondie   105 calories • 6 g fat • 8 g carbs • 3 g fiber • 6 g protein

Per muffin   168 calories • 9 g fat • 12 g carbs • 5 g fiber • 9 g protein

Nourishment Breakdown

PROTEIN powder
FAT nut butter, dark chocolate

FIBER coconut flour
CARB/STARCH potato/pumpkin

Berry Sorbet

A good choice for a high-quality carb/starch dessert or a blood sugar friendly snack thanks to the protein in the yogurt. Berries are loaded with minerals and vitamins like potassium, magnesium, vitamins C and K, fiber, and prebiotics. Frozen berries are usually frozen at peak season so you can get the health benefits of fresh berries all year long.

2 cups (290 g) frozen berries
½ cup (120 ml) water
1 cup (230 g) plain nonfat or
    full-fat Greek yogurt
2 teaspoons lemon juice
2 tablespoons (16 g) monk
    fruit, allulose, or desired
    sweetener, optional

Blend all ingredients on low in the blender or food processor until well combined.

Pour into a shallow dish with a lid.

Cover and freeze 2 to 3 hours until set. If you store for longer, you'll need to let it sit on counter to soften before serving.

Per serving   54 calories • 0 g fat • 8 g carbs • 3 g fiber • 4 g protein

Nourishment Breakdown

PROTEIN small amount in yogurt
FAT none or yogurt, if using full-fat

FIBER some in berries
CARB/STARCH berries

Quick Mug Cake

When your sweet tooth is calling and you need a single-serve, feel-good dessert, fast . . . this is the recipe for you! The macro balance differs depending on the flour you choose. I use coconut flour (lower fat) if it's for a dessert after a higher fat meal and almond flour (more fat) for a more filling snack or a meal in itself. You can switch up the flavors with different protein powders. This recipe is for a blood sugar balanced version of a yellow cake and chocolate icing, an American classic.

½ cup (125 g) unsweetened
    applesauce
1 egg or flax egg
Dash salt
¼ teaspoon vanilla extract
3 tablespoons (21 g) almond
    flour or 1 tablespoon (6 g)
    coconut flour
2 tablespoons (16 g) vanilla
    protein powder
¼ teaspoon baking powder

In a sprayed large coffee mug or cereal bowl, combine ingredients in the order listed.

Stir well and microwave for 1 minute. Let the batter settle so it won't overflow. Continue cooking for 30 seconds to 2 minutes total depending on the texture you prefer.

While it cools, make the chocolate icing.

Per serving with almond flour and icing
350 calories • 15 g fat • 17 g carbs • 5 g fiber • 25 g protein
Per serving with coconut flour and icing
230 calories • 4 g fat • 16 g carbs • 6 g fiber • 22 g protein

Nourishment Breakdown
PROTEIN powder, egg
FAT egg or flax if using, almond flour, dark chips
FIBER none or coconut flour
CARB/STARCH applesauce

Chocolate Icing

2 tablespoons (22 g) dark
    chocolate chips

Microwave chocolate in a glass bowl for 1 minute. They may not look melted but don't overcook.

Remove and stir well until smooth and pour over the prepared cake.

Lemon Chia Protein Cookies

Light and crumbly, these cookies are delicious. Each one contains protein, fat, and fiber to keep your blood sugar happy whether you eat it as a dessert or a snack.

⅓ cup (35 g) almond flour

½ cup (45 g) coconut flour

⅓ cup (72 g) unflavored collagen

3 tablespoons (45 g) monk fruit/ or allulose blend

1 teaspoon baking powder

1 tablespoon (11 g) chia seeds

¼ cup (55 g) butter, melted

½ cup (120 ml) almond milk

1 teaspoon vanilla extract

1 egg

1 tablespoon (6 g) lemon zest

3 tablespoons (45 ml) lemon juice

Preheat oven to 350°F (180°C, or gas mark 4).

In a large bowl, combine flours, collagen, monk fruit, baking powder, and chia seeds. Stir to combine.

In a medium bowl, add remaining ingredients and stir to combine.

Add wet ingredients to dry and stir until combined.

Form into 1½-inch (3.5-cm) cookie shapes on a sprayed cookie sheet. Bake for 12 to 14 minutes.

Allow to cool before moving. Store in the fridge.

Per cookie   90 calories • 7 g fat • 35 g carbs • 2 g fiber • 5 g protein

Nourishment Breakdown

PROTEIN collagen

FAT butter, almond flour, egg

FIBER coconut flour

CARB/STARCH none

Cookie Dough Protein Fudge

If you're a chocoholic, this recipe is for you. More good news? Dark chocolate contains plant compounds that act as antioxidants. I often prep this dish ahead of time, so I always have it on hand for a blood sugar balanced dessert or a snack. If you're using a plant-based protein powder, skip the coconut flour to make it less chalky and dry and give it a better texture. I use whey or beef protein powder.

7 ounces (200 g) white chocolate chips, preferably stevia sweetened

¼ cup (32 g) vanilla protein powder

2 tablespoons (12 g) coconut flour

½ teaspoon vanilla extract

Dash of pink salt

¼ cup (44 g) dark chocolate chips

In a glass bowl, microwave chocolate chips for 1 minute. They won't look melted but stir to make smooth. Don't overcook. It will make the mixture too thick.

Add all other ingredients except the dark chips and stir.

Press into a lined bread pan and add chocolate chips to the top. Press lightly into fudge.

Refrigerate for an hour or so to set. Cut into desired squares. Store in the fridge or freezer.

Per 1-inch piece   62 calories • 4 g fat • 9 g carbs • 3 g fiber • 2 g protein

Nourishment Breakdown

PROTEIN powder

FAT chocolate

FIBER coconut flour

CARB/STARCH some in chocolate

Chewy Peanut Butter Cookies

Loaded with healthy fiber, fats, and collagen protein, this makes a balanced snack, dessert, or a topping for yogurt or a smoothie. Even chewier and yummier on the second day after they've been in the fridge overnight.

DRY INGREDIENTS

⅓ cup (72 g) unflavored collagen protein

½ cup (78 g) oats (can be gluten-free if needed)

⅓ cup (60 g) coconut flour

¼ cup (32 g) monk fruit or allulose blend granulated sweetener

¼ teaspoon pink salt

WET INGREDIENTS

⅓ cup (86 g) peanut butter (natural or organic with peanuts and salt as the only ingredients)

1 teaspoon vanilla extract

¼ cup (60 ml) almond milk

Preheat oven to 350°F (180°C, or gas mark 4).

Combine dry ingredients in a large bowl and stir.

Add wet ingredients and stir well.

Dough will be sticky but it's worth it for the chewy cookie factor.

Form into 1½-inch (3.5-cm) cookies and press to make cookie shape. Bake for 12 to 14 minutes. Let cookies sit for 20 minutes to cool and set.

Per cookie   86 calories • 45 g fat • 6 g carbs • 3 g fiber • 7 g protein

Nourishment Breakdown

PROTEIN collagen

FAT peanut butter

FIBER coconut flour

CARB/STARCH oats

12

Meal Plan Options

THIS IS A gentle structured weekly guide for a month of meal prep to make changing your eating habits easier. For me, Sunday is a prep day, but choose a day that works for your schedule and week. These are all simple recipes, so it's only about 1 to 2 hours maximum of prep time in the kitchen. If you enjoy naturally sweet desserts or snacks on a regular basis, prep these dishes too.

I suggest that you buy the ingredients to cook dinner for three nights and fill in with leftovers, eating out, or ordering in. Make sure that you stock up each week on the ingredients for smoothies and have simple proteins like canned tuna and cottage cheese on hand to use in recipes as needed.

In our house, Friday evenings are BYOM (build your own meal) or we eat dinner out. On Saturdays, you can also BYOM, dine out, or order in.

Week One

	BREAKFAST	LUNCH	DINNER	DESSERT
SUNDAY	Pesto Protein Egg Muffins (page 34)	Dill Chicken Salad (page 92)	Balanced Meal Chili (page 110) *or* rotisserie chicken to go with Gorgonzola Pear Salad (page 156) *or* Carnitas Power Bowls (page 135)	Peanut Butter Blondie Muffins (page 175)
MONDAY	Pesto Protein Egg Muffins (page 34) and fruit	Dill Chicken Salad (page 92) on a low-carb tortilla or with crackers	Leftover Balanced Meal Chili (page 110)	{none}
TUESDAY	Glowing Skin Smoothie (page 67)	Pesto Protein Egg Muffins (page 34) and a piece of toast	Leftover Meal Chili (page 110) *or* Chicken Salad (page 90)	{none}
WEDNESDAY	Pesto Protein Egg Muffins (page 34)	Banana Cream Pie Yogurt Bowl (page 43) *or* Dill Chicken Salad (page 92)	Carnitas Power Bowls (page 135)	{none}
THURSDAY	Warm Peanut Butter & Jelly Protein Bowl (page 49)	Leftover Carnitas Power Bowls (page 135)	Rotisserie chicken and Gorgonzola Pear Salad (page 156)	{none}
FRIDAY	Pesto Protein Egg Muffins (page 34) *or* Snickers Smoothie (page 75)	Any leftovers *or* Savory Protein Toast (page 93)	BYOM *or* dinner out	{none}

Week Two

	BREAKFAST	LUNCH	DINNER	DESSERT
SUNDAY	Basic Overnight Oatmeal (page 48) *or* N'Oatmeal (page 47)	High-Protein Pimento Cheese (page 82)	Mediterranean Beef Stew (page 116) *or* Balanced Basic Taco Night (page 122) *or* Chicken Spinach Artichoke Bake (page 106)	No-Bake Buckeyes (page 168)
MONDAY	Basic Overnight Oatmeal (page 48) *or* N'Oatmeal (page 47)	High-Protein Pimento Cheese (page 82) with seeded crackers	Chicken Spinach Artichoke Bake (page 106)	{none}
TUESDAY	Basic Overnight Oatmeal (page 48) *or* N'Oatmeal (page 47)	Leftover Chicken Bake *or* High-Protein Pimento Cheese (page 82)	Balanced Basic Taco Night (page 122) *or* leftovers	{none}
WEDNESDAY	Turmeric Veggie Scramble (page 39)	Leftover Tacos *or* High-Protein Pimento Cheese (page 82)	Smoothie of choice *or* Single-Serve Chocolate Cookie (page 167)	{none}
THURSDAY	Basic Overnight Oatmeal (page 48) *or* N'Oatmeal (page 47)	Tuna Quesadilla (page 85)	Leftover Mediterranean Beef Stew (page 116)	{none}
FRIDAY	Raspberries & Cream Smoothie (page 70)	Leftover Mediterranean Stew (page 116)	BYOM *or* dinner out	{none}

Week Three

	BREAKFAST	LUNCH	DINNER	DESSERT
SUNDAY	Breakfast Meatballs (page 36)	Tuna Salad (page 91) *or* Sriracha Salmon Power Bowls (page 132)	Chicken Philly Sheet Pan (page 123) *or* Rosemary Pot Roast (page 96)	Cookie Dough Protein Fudge (page 181)
MONDAY	Breakfast Meatballs (page 36) with fruit	Tuna Salad (page 91) in a low-carb wrap or on a salad *or* Carrot Cake Protein Toast (page 83)	Sriracha Salmon Power Bowls (page 132)	{none}
TUESDAY	Cinnamon Toast Smoothie (page 76)	Breakfast Meatballs (page 36) with toast	Leftover Sriracha Salmon Power Bowls (page 132) *or* Chicken Philly Sheet Pan (page 123)	{none}
WEDNESDAY	Breakfast Meatballs (page 36) *or* smoothie of choice	Tuna Salad (page 91) or leftovers	Rosemary Pot Roast (page 96) *or* leftovers	{none}
THURSDAY	Sweet or Savory Cottage Cheese Bowl (page 54)	Quick Mug Frittata (page 41) *or* leftovers	Leftovers or BYOM	{none}
FRIDAY	Sugar Cookie Warm Protein Bowl (page 53)	Leftovers	BYOM *or* dinner out	{none}

Week Four

	BREAKFAST	LUNCH	DINNER	DESSERT
SUNDAY	Protein Cheesecake Parfait (page 33)	Sloppy Joe Power Bowls (page 134)	Balanced Breakfast Casserole (page 55) *or* Zuppa Toscana (page 113) *or* Italian Stuffed Peppers (page 104)	Lemon Chia Protein Cookies (page 179)
MONDAY	Protein Cheesecake Parfait (page 33)	Sloppy Joe Power Bowls (page 134)	Balanced Breakfast Casserole (page 55) with fruit	{none}
TUESDAY	Protein Cheesecake Parfait (page 33)	Leftover Balanced Breakfast Casserole (page 55)	Sloppy Joe Power Bowls (page 134)	{none}
WEDNESDAY	Almond Joy Smoothie (page 69)	Savory Protein Veggie Dip (page 86) *or* leftover Breakfast Casserole (page 55)	Zuppa Toscana (page 113)	{none}
THURSDAY	Basic Vanilla Smoothie (page 64)	Leftover Zuppa Toscana (page 113)	Italian Stuffed Peppers (page 104)	{none}
FRIDAY	Sweet Potato Protein Bowl (page 52)	Leftovers *or* Tuna Quesadilla (page 85)	BYOM or dinner out	{none}

ABOUT THE AUTHOR

Meredith Mann is the creator of the Instagram and TikTok handles @thepeachiespoon. She is a certified holistic nutrition coach and CPT specializing in metabolism, blood sugar regulation, and emotional eating.

ACKNOWLEDGMENTS

I want to express my deep gratitude to the wonderful community on my Peachie Spoon Instagram page. Your unwavering support, recipe requests, constructive criticism, and daily affirmations have fueled my journey in creating this cookbook. Without your passion for healthy cooking and dedication, this project wouldn't have been possible.

To my incredible husband and business partner, Eric, your constant support and encouragement have been a true blessing. You are my rock, and I am grateful for every moment we share together.

To my daughter, Lydia, watching you explore the kitchen and embrace new recipes fills me with joy. Thank you for being my enthusiastic sous chef and grocery store companion.

To my sons, Carson and Crawford, your voracious teenage appetites and willingness to experiment with my recipes have inspired me so much. Thank you for the extra smoothie-making practice every afternoon because you love them as much as me. You've both made me appreciate the understanding of allergies and dietary restrictions many families face so we can all enjoy the same meal together as a family.

To my parents, thank you for your unwavering support and encouragement. Dad, your words of wisdom and encouragement mean the world to me. Mom, your love for creating a warm and cozy home environment has left a lasting impression on me and my own family.

To my siblings, Lindsey and Trevor, your own journeys towards healthier lifestyles and your constant support mean everything to me. So thankful for our daily chats, Linz.

To my team at Quarto, Jill, you held my hand through each stage of creating this book and you made it so doable and not overwhelming. Working with you all has been a dream.

And to Virginia, a heartfelt thank you for your thorough reviews and dedication to our mission of promoting simple, nutritious meals. Your contributions have made this cookbook even better.

INDEX